# Women's Golf

# Women's Golf

**Nick Wright**

hamlyn

First published in Great Britain in 2002 by Hamlyn, a division of
Octopus Publishing Group Ltd, 2–4 Heron Quays, London E14 4JP

Copyright © Octopus Publishing Group Ltd 2002

Distributed in the United States and Canada by
Sterling Publishing Co., Inc.
387 Park Avenue South, New York, NY10016–8810

ISBN 0 600 60421 7

A CIP catalogue record for this book is available from the British Library

Printed and bound in China

10 9 8 7 6 5 4 3 2 1

All photographs in this book were taken on location at the
**East Sussex National Golf Club** and **Woburn Golf Club**.

**Measurements**
Throughout *Women's Golf* distances are quoted in yards, still in use
throughout most of the UK, the USA and Japan. In many other countries
metres are standard. The difference (less than one per cent) may not seem
great, but it is enough to make a difference of one club at 100 yards. To
convert to metres multiply the yardage by 0.9144.

**Publisher's note**
The text has been written from the point-of-view of teaching a right-
handed player. Reverse the advice given for left-handed players to read
'left' for 'right' and vice versa.

# Contents

# Foreword

**C**asting my eye back over the development of women's golf during the past quarter of a century, I think it is fair to say that the game has changed beyond all recognition since I was a full-time Tour player in the 1970s. I played most of my golf in America in those days and they were great times. Although most of the players were far from household names, it was fantastic just to be involved in the pioneering stage of women's golf when the television networks and the media were just beginning to show an interest in the sport. I think we all knew we were starting something very special.

Some 30 years on, the game has progressed immeasurably. I can remember the time when Judy Rankin became the first player to win $100,000 in a season. Today, the world's top stars will earn well over $2m.

One of the most pleasing developments as far as I am concerned is that women's golf now has such a global appeal. Although the LPGA Tour in America remains the world's most lucrative Tour, the most dominant players over the past few seasons – Australia's Karrie Webb, Sweden's Annika Sorenstam and Korea's Se Ri Pak – come from three different continents.

I have obviously been delighted to see the quality of golf in Europe improve by leaps and bounds over the past decade or so and that has been reflected in some fantastic Solheim Cup duels with the Americans in recent years. Despite the great times I enjoyed as a player, nothing has come close to the experiences of captaining the European side between 1990 and 1996.

Words alone can never fully describe the emotions that you go through after losing a closely fought team encounter or the sheer relief, elation and euphoria that accompanies a winning performance – but needless to say I wouldn't have traded any of those experiences for anything and I will always look back on the matches with a great deal of pride and satisfaction. I just hope that the passion and spirit demonstrated by players on both the European and American teams continue to attract newcomers to the game.

Whether it is played in an individual or team format, golf is a fantastic sport and with the opportunities for women in golf constantly improving there is no better time than the present to get out onto the fairways and sample the joys and frustrations of the game for yourself. I know you won't be disappointed.

Good luck, good playing and enjoy the game.

Mickey Walker

# *Introduction*

**G**olf has enjoyed something of a boom period during the past four or five years, and much of this success can be attributed to the contribution of one man: Tiger Woods. The American superstar has attracted millions of youngsters to a game that they would ordinarily have ignored in favour of higher profile sports, such as basketball and baseball in America, and soccer in Europe and Asia.

One might expect the majority of these newcomers to be teenage boys who identify with Woods' swashbuckling style of play, but the explosion in golf's popularity has also seen a marked increase in the number of girls taking up the sport. All of a sudden, after years of being associated with middle-aged men in garish knitwear and hideous check trousers, golf has become a cool sport to youngsters of both sexes across the world.

However, despite the huge numbers of adolescents currently taking up the game, women's golf remains the fastest-growing section of the sport. Today, top women professionals enjoy celebrity status, lead increasingly glamorous lifestyles and compete for big prize money, and it is a trend that looks set to continue for many years to come.

Golf is a sport that has been accused, quite rightly at times, of elitism, racism and sexism. Unfortunately, if you look hard enough you will still find golf clubs with prejudiced views toward various sectors of our society. However, I am also delighted to say that in my experience of visiting many hundreds of golf clubs around the world, a wind of change has swept through the golf industry in the past decade. Previously unhelpful and unaccommodating, golf clubs have suddenly begun to adopt a more tolerant and welcoming attitude to all golfers, regardless of their gender, the colour of their skin or the size of their bank balance.

I am sure that it is too idealistic to suggest that this process of liberalization has been the result of some deep soul-searching. Unfortunately, it is far more likely to have been prompted by the commercial pressures of a competitive market. To put it simply, golf clubs have cast their net wider to attract business and have relaxed their admissions procedures to retain existing levels of memberships. But whatever the reason, it is still encouraging to see juniors, women, and people of all races and income levels given an equal opportunity to play the game of golf.

*Nick Wright*

# Women's Golf in the 21st Century

**T**oday, in the first decade of the 21st century, women's golf is booming like never before. More and more young girls are choosing to take up the sport, golf clubs around the world are becoming increasingly accommodating and the top golfers on the world stage are competing for bigger and better prizes.

Whereas the women's tour was once regarded by many as inferior to the men's, anyone who has attended a Ladies' Professional Golf Association (LPGA) Tour event in recent years can only have been impressed by the way many modern women golfers strike the ball. They play with confidence, hit the ball powerfully and shoot low scores. Women's golf's current superstars, such as Annika Sorenstam and Karrie Webb, have become household names alongside the likes of David Duval and Phil Mickelson, and there is no reason that the increase in popularity of the women's game cannot continue for many years to come.

# Women's golf: the key issues

*Left:* **While many women golfers have excellent rhythm, it is important to remember that you still have to hit the ball authoritatively.**

readers sounds obvious, but it often needs saying nonetheless: to hit the ball a long way you have to hit it *hard*.

Many women are often applauded for their rhythmical swings. Unlike most men, who cannot resist lunging at the ball in a misguided attempt to scramble a few extra yards, the majority of women swing at an even tempo back and through. However, while this action may look good, it does not in itself generate much power or distance. Watch any of the top players on television – Karrie Webb, Se Ri Pak and Maria Hjorth immediately spring to mind – and you will see that even though they all have a smooth, unhurried rhythm, they also give the ball a good thump through impact.

The key is turning on the power at the right time within the confines of a rhythmical swing. In the downswing the build-up of power should be gradual as the clubhead approaches the ball. Problems occur in the golf swing when you change speed and direction suddenly. As long as you build up to a positive hit through impact, there is no reason why you should lose your rhythm or your timing as you hit the ball.

## The chest issue

The other significant difference between men's and women's golf is also a physical one. While men can freely swing their arms away from the ball on the backswing, many women find that their chest restricts this movement and causes problems with their technique and timing.

Just how much your chest will interfere with your swing obviously depends on the size of your bust. Women with smaller chests will find that their backswing is less restricted than women whose chests present a greater obstacle.

Opinions vary on how best to overcome this problem, but the general consensus is that if you have a small to regular-sized bust, you should set up with your arms to the side of your chest and squeeze in gently. If, however, your bust is larger than average, you should let your arms rest on top of your chest and simply allow your upper body to go with the flow as you turn back and through.

## Creating a powerful swing

The greatest difference between men and women golfers is power. Men are naturally stronger and will therefore be able to hit the ball further than most women. Playing from the red tees will help many women golfers compensate for much of the difference, but the fact remains that most women do not get as much power out of their swing as they could.

In my capacities as the instruction editor on both *Golf Monthly* and *Women & Golf*, the majority of letters that I receive from women request advice on improving their distance off the tee and from the fairway. The advice I give our

**1** Many women make the mistake of resting their arms on top of their chest to minimize interference on their swing, but it is better to let your arms hang to the sides. By doing this, the whole of your upper body and your arms can turn together in the backswing and downswing.

**2** Once you have positioned your arms to the side of your chest, bring both arms in to form your grip. If you do this correctly you should find that you gently squeeze your chest inwards.

## PLAYING GOLF WHILE PREGNANT

In the Women's US Open championship in 2001, a competitor played the first two rounds of the tournament while nine month's pregnant. While that should not be regarded as a green light for every expectant mother to continue playing golf right up until they go into labour, it does highlight the fact that, unless you have been advised otherwise by a doctor, there is no reason why you should stop playing golf as soon as you discover that you are pregnant.

Each individual will have their own cut-off date, depending on their health and fitness, but as a rule you can continue playing golf while pregnant as long as it does not cause distress or discomfort. It is, however, a good idea to ask your doctor for advice on how often you can play and for how long into your pregnancy.

# Learning to play

## Professional tuition

Regular lessons will greatly aid your development as a golfer, so choosing the right professional to teach you is a major decision, and one that should be made sooner rather than later. Many beginners fall into the trap of thinking that, like the different brands of golf balls, all golf pros are essentially the same. That could not be further from the truth. While most golf pros will be experienced teachers, some are better communicators than others and have more interest in the subject. The ideal golf coach is one who gains a great deal of satisfaction out of watching you improve, who has an infectious passion for the game and who gets as much enjoyment out of each lesson as you do.

There are plenty of women teaching professionals today, but selecting a coach on the basis of gender can be ill advised.

A better idea is to find a golf professional who specializes in teaching women. It is also sensible to opt for a coach who is experienced in teaching players of your level. Some teachers enjoy coaching beginners, others prefer to work with lower handicap golfers while a few coaches choose only to work with club and tournament professionals. It is always a good idea to ask friends and family for personal referrals rather than picking up the phone book and ringing the first entry listed under the 'golf professional' category.

### Things to consider

The most important criteria when selecting an instructor are his or her attitude and their approach to teaching. Just as in any learning environment, personality plays a key role in golf tuition. If your instructor makes the lessons entertaining and enjoyable and also shows a genuine personal interest in your improvement, you are likely to progress far quicker than if the lesson experience is dull and uninspiring. There is, similarly, nothing worse than the teacher struggling to remember your name and having to spend the first part of each lesson familiarizing themselves with your game and trying to remember what subjects they covered in your previous lesson.

Finally, always remember that if you do not notice an improvement in your game or handicap after a series of regular lessons, do not hesitate to change your instructor. Amazingly, many amateur golfers continue to take lessons month after month and, occasionally, year after year without showing any signs of a significant improvement. You would not continue to take driving lessons if your road skills were not getting any better, so why should your golf be any different?

Teaching professionals know that they are judged on results and they should understand your decision not to continue with lessons if you are not satisfied with the progress you are making under their tutelage.

*Left:* **Regular tuition from a qualified golf professional or instructor is by far the quickest and most effective way to learn and improve your golf.**

# Out on the course

Your first few rounds of golf will undoubtedly be nervy and tentative affairs. It is not easy to leave the comfort of the lesson tee and the driving range for the unforgiving and punishing golf course. Although it is advisable to have several lessons and plenty of sessions at the range to build your confidence first, it is important to get out and start playing for real as soon as is feasibly possible. It is only on the golf course that you will learn the art of managing your game and the subtle skills that cannot be acquired on a driving range. Even the most advanced practice facility cannot compete with the golf course as a learning ground for new players.

While learning the ropes, you should always try to play with more experienced golfers who will be happy to explain the correct golfing etiquette, rules and behaviour as you go round. Avoid golfers who become frustrated and bad-tempered if you struggle to play certain shots.

On the golf course, you will notice that there are several different tee areas on each hole. In almost all cases, the ladies tee will be coloured red. The red tees are normally positioned ahead of the men's tees and the championship tees. The general idea is that, because most women do not hit the ball as far as most men, the red tees are placed further forward to allow men and women to hit their approach shots into the green with roughly the same club. Other than that, women do not benefit from any positive discrimination in the rules, and once your tee shot is out of the way, you are on an equal footing with the men.

*Left:* **Even if you are a complete beginner, it is still a good idea to get out onto the golf course and start playing as soon as possible.**

## JOINING A GOLF CLUB

If your long-term goal is to obtain a handicap and play in official competitions, you will at some stage need to join a golf club. Thanks to the emergence of many new commercially-minded golf courses, this is a far easier process for women today than it was 20 years ago. Up until fairly recently, women members of many old-style private golf clubs were treated almost like second-class citizens and given limited access to the golf course and the clubhouse. Sadly, there are still a few antiquated private members' clubs that operate under their own house rules and refuse to even entertain the idea of accepting women as members. Fortunately, recent legislation from Europe regarding human rights and equal opportunities means that women now enjoy the same playing and membership privileges as the men at many golf courses around the world.

If you are thinking of joining a golf club, it is highly likely that you will already have one in mind, probably your local course or one where several friends already play. However, it is still worth carrying out a little research to ensure that the golf club is the right one for you before you commit yourself to paying what can be a sizeable joining fee and annual subscription.

Many private golf clubs will ask you to attend an interview with the club committee before they grant you membership, and this is also your chance to quiz the members about how the club operates. Find out how the women members are treated, if there are any restrictions on tee times, whether the club runs an equal rights policy and whether there are any restrictions on the number of guests you can sign in to play during the course of a year. You can also ask about the social activities and enquire about any other facilities that the club may have to offer. All of the above questions will help you discover whether you are right for the club and, of course, vice versa.

# Equipment

## Choosing your first set of clubs

In today's modern, competitive market, manufacturing standards have improved to such a level that it is almost impossible to find a poor set of golf clubs. Long gone are the days when reputable brand name manufacturers were few and far between, and when a golf retailer's idea of a ladies' range would have been a token set hidden among the cobwebs in a broom cupboard at the back of the shop.

Today the choice of golf clubs available to the woman player is remarkable and, contrary to popular belief, you do not have to pay a fortune to kit yourself out. Obviously, some clubs are assembled using more durable and expensive components than others, and that will be reflected in the price but, by and large, even inexpensive clubs perform well today.

*Right:* **A typical modern set of women's clubs includes a range of several fairway woods and cavity-backed irons to make the game easier and more fun to play.**

*Below:* **Together with your golf clubs, you will need to carry a wide range of accessories in your golf bag.**

The initial outlay for getting started in golf can be expensive, but if purchased and used correctly, your golf clubs will last for many years. Even with regular cleaning, shoes, gloves and waterproofs inevitably get old and shabby, but if you care for your clubs they will look like new for many years.

If you are an absolute beginner, there is no need to jump in and buy the most expensive set of clubs available. For the first few years, while you are learning to play, you will not be able to notice the slightest difference between a cheap set and a top-of-the-range set. Many companies now offer beginners' sets with an option of trading up to a more advanced set in the future. You can also purchase an initial starter set of four or five key clubs and add to the set as your game improves. Here are a few tips on selecting your first set.

### Renew grips once a year

Out of all the components that make up a golf club, the grip is the one that wears out the quickest. If you play a lot of golf, it is inevitable that your grips will wear down and become smooth and shiny. When this happens, it becomes difficult to maintain control of the club during your swing.

The world's top players will often change their grips every month or so, but unless you play several times each week that is an unnecessary extravagance for most golfers. Ideally, you should renew your grips at the start of each season. Your local club professional will be able to do this for you.

## Choose cavity-backed clubs

It is likely that your first set of clubs will be what is known as 'cavity-backed'. Also known as perimeter-weighting, this term refers to a particular manufacturing process where weight is scooped out of the back of the club and redistributed around the edges. Most top professionals use cavity-backed clubs these days because they are more forgiving and easier to use.

You may also be given the option of purchasing a set of 'bladed' clubs. As the name suggests, the clubhead is simply a thin strip of forged metal. These traditional style clubs are still popular with some of the die-hards on the professional Tours, but they are becoming less and less popular among amateurs and professionals because they have a smaller sweetspot and are, therefore, more difficult to use.

## Selecting the correct shaft flex

As any manufacturer will tell you, the shaft is by far the most important component of the golf club. Its characteristics will influence the height, shape and trajectory of your shots and the amount of swing speed you can generate.

Shaft production is a scientific process and manufacturers constantly experiment with different materials and alloys to produce shafts with a range of strengths and flexes. However, do not get too carried away with technology. The only factor the novice needs to consider is the shaft flex. Quite simply, this indicates how much the shaft will bend during the swing. Strong golfers and low handicappers, who generate a lot of clubhead speed, will need to use a stiffer shaft than a less athletic or higher handicap golfer, who will need extra flex to help compensate for their lack of swing speed and power.

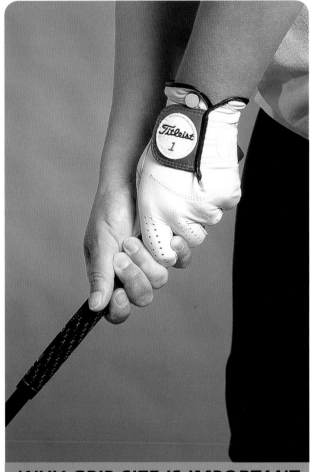

## WHY GRIP SIZE IS IMPORTANT

Grip thickness is an important equipment issue that is all too often overlooked by players. To ignore it is a big mistake, since if your grips are either too thin or too thick for the size of your hands, you will struggle to swing the club correctly.

Grips that are too thin, for example, will cause you to develop too much hand action in your swing, while grips that are too thick will restrict your wrist action during the swing, thereby diminishing the power and accuracy of the shot. When holding a golf club, the tips of your fingers should just touch the base of your thumb pad. Most manufacturers offer a wide range of grip sizes, so do not be afraid to try a few samples before committing to a purchase.

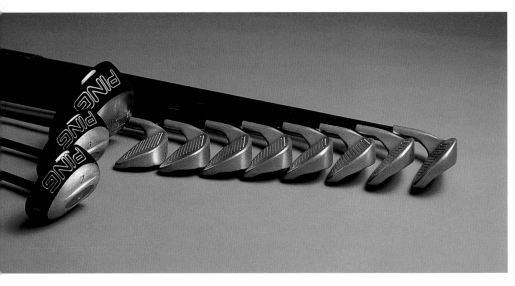

*Left:* Most manufacturers produce a wide range of fairway woods and irons, but you are only allowed to carry 14 clubs in your bag at any one time.

*Below:* Since well over half the strokes that you play during a round of golf will be taken on the green, it makes sense to choose your putter carefully.

## Choosing your set make-up

Once you have selected a brand and model of golf club, your next step is to decide on the composition of your set. Most manufacturers produce at least six fairway woods, up to 13 irons and a putter, giving you 20 different clubs to choose from. However, the rules of golf restrict you to carrying just 14 in your bag at any one time, so you need to think very carefully indeed about which clubs you should include.

### Irons or woods?

Your golf professional or retailer should be able to give you some helpful advice on which clubs will enable you to get the most out of your game. Many women find that they benefit from replacing some of the longer irons with the easier-to-hit fairway woods. Sweden's Annika Sorenstam started this trend on Tour several years ago, when she ditched her 3-iron, 4-iron and 5-iron and replaced them with a 5-wood, 7-wood and 9-wood. Although some of the more traditional players still persist with their longer irons, many professionals have now realized the benefits of a range of fairway woods.

### Wedges

Most golf manufacturers also produce a range of up to four different types of wedge. In addition to the regular sand wedge and pitching wedge, you also have the option of adding a lob wedge or a gap wedge to your bag. The lob wedge is a lofted club and allows you to play some more adventurous shots around the green, while the gap wedge fills the 'gap' between your pitching wedge and sand wedge. Ask your golf professional how best to compile your set.

## QUICK TIP

### Avoid using men's clubs

With the exception of some of the stronger women professional golfers, it is not a good idea to learn or play using men's clubs. The main reason for this is that, because men are generally taller and stronger, the shafts fitted to their clubs are longer and stiffer. This makes it difficult to generate clubhead speed at impact if you are not physically strong enough. However, it is also true to say that many men would benefit from switching to ladies' clubs. The shorter club length improves control, while the extra flexibility in the shafts helps to increase power.

# A well-fitting putter

Out of all the clubs in your bag, the putter is the one you will use most during a round of golf. Your putter should complement your physique, posture and putting style so that you feel comfortable when using it.

Many golfers make the mistake of adapting their posture to suit their putter, but that can lead to all manner of contorted positions and poor shots. The correct putter for you is one that allows you to maintain a comfortable and relaxed posture with your eyes directly above the ball.

If the putter shaft is too long, for example, you are likely to stand too upright at address. If the shaft is too short, you may find that you have to bend forwards excessively to reach the grip. The lie of the putter is also important. If the lie is too upright, the toe of the putter may point in the air. If the lie is too shallow, the heel of the club may be raised. Neither is conducive to consistent putting. If the putter lies correctly you should just be able to slide a small coin under the toe of the club at address.

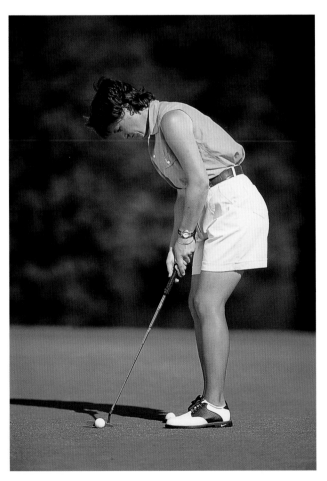

*Left:* A custom-fit putter will enable you to set up correctly with your eyes directly over the ball at address.

## JARGON-BUSTER

When purchasing a set of clubs you may come across some confusing technical jargon.

### Cavity-back
A style of clubhead design where most of the weight is distributed around the edges of the club, leaving a hollow cavity at the back that increases the size of the sweet spot.

### Blade
A traditional style of design, where the clubface is forged from a thin strip of steel. These clubs offer increased feel but are less forgiving than cavity-backs.

### Loft
The angle of the clubface determines how high or low the ball will fly. For maximum distance, drivers start at about seven or eight degrees, while some lob wedges have up to 64 degrees of loft.

### Grooves
These are scores in the clubface designed to create friction when the ball is struck, thereby generating backspin.

### Shaft flex
This is the amount that a shaft bends during the swing. Good players, who create a lot of clubhead speed, generally use stiff shafts, while beginners and higher handicappers who are not so powerful, will benefit from more flexible shafts.

### Graphite
A strong, lightweight material which is often used as an alternative to steel in shafts. The lighter club weight enables the golfer to generate more clubhead speed. Senior golfers also benefit from graphite's vibration absorption qualities.

### Torque
As well as flexing during the swing, a shaft also twists. Shafts with excessive torque can produce inconsistent results.

# Accessories, balls and shoes

In addition to your golf clubs, there is a whole range of accessories that you will need to take with you to the golf course. The first and most obvious is a golf bag to put everything in. Modern golf bags are lightweight, well-designed and stylish, with plenty of compartments for you to carry many different items. If you plan to carry your bag rather than use a motorized or pull trolley, it is a good idea to select one that has a dual strap system that slips over both shoulders. This spreads the weight evenly across your back and reduces the possibility of injury.

Make sure that your bag is also fitted with a stand. Many modern bags have spring-loaded stands that pop out automatically when the bag is placed on the ground. If your bag has a stand, you will not have to lay it on the ground in wet weather. It sounds trivial, but when you pick up a wet bag, water will run down the clubs to the grips, making them wet and difficult to hold properly. It will also soak your clothes, making for an uncomfortable round.

## Golf balls

If you are a beginner, there is little point purchasing the most expensive brand of golf balls. Until you can strike the ball consistently, you will not be able to tell the difference between a top-of-the-range branded ball and an X-out. However, once your swing becomes reasonably consistent you can select a golf ball to match your game. Manufacturing technology is so advanced now that all the major golf ball companies can produce a ball that reaches the maximum speed restrictions imposed by the game's governing bodies.

However, at the end of the day there is always a trade-off between distance and control. You can opt for one or the other or a combination of the two. Many beginners and less powerful players are willing to sacrifice a little touch and feel around the greens for the extra distance offered by a golf ball with a solid cover. Golf professionals, lower handicappers and strong players often prefer to use a golf ball that gives them enhanced feel around the greens rather than extra distance.

*Left:* Many modern golf bags are well-designed, lightweight and feature a special strap system that reduces the risk of damaging your back.

*Below:* The modern golf ball is durable and offers a good combination of distance and control for all players.

*Above:* Today's lightweight golf shoes are a stylish addition to the golfer's range of clothing.

*Left:* The clubhead, shaft and grip all influence the performance of the club and your shots.

## Golf gloves

Golf gloves are intended to help you grip the club more securely with your left hand (right hand for left-handed players) and reduce the chances of the club slipping out of position during your swing. Most top players wear their glove for hitting full shots, but take it off occasionally for chipping and pitching and almost always for putting, when they believe they will have more feel without it.

## Golf shoes

Once again, manufacturing standards are so high these days that you are spoilt for choice when choosing shoes. Many golfers have a pair of waterproof shoes for the wet winter months and a pair of lightweight shoes for the dry summer season, although it is possible to purchase lightweight waterproof shoes.

Most shoes these days are supplied fitted with soft spikes, which perform well in all weather conditions. These spikes are more environmentally friendly, as they do not leave indentations in the greens and damage the putting surface.

## Preparing for wet weather

Playing golf in the rain can be a thoroughly unpleasant experience if you do not have the necessary accessories. You should always take a waterproof suit and an umbrella to the golf course, unless you are playing in a climate where you can guarantee that there will be no rainfall.

When choosing a waterproof suit, select one that is 'breathable' as well as 100 per cent waterproof. Many modern materials allow air to escape from the suit through tiny perforations, while preventing the larger water droplets from getting in. Some suits also have a windproof liner.

Another essential accessory is a large golf towel or, preferably, several small towels that you can use to keep your grips dry and your clubs clean during the round.

## GOLF BAG CHECKLIST

Aside from the basic equipment, before you step onto the first tee it is important to check the following:

- You are carrying a pitchmark repairer, a pencil, towel(s), waterproofs, an umbrella, a glove, a scorecard, a snack and water, a woolly hat, a hand warmer

- You are carrying a maximum of 14 clubs
- You have marked your golf balls
- You are aware of local rules

# The pioneers of women's golf

Just as players such as Bobby Jones, Arnold Palmer, Jack Nicklaus and Tiger Woods have raised the profile of men's golf, so there are several female golfers who should be credited for doing the very same thing for the women's game.

## Babe Zaharias

Regarded by many as the greatest woman athlete in history, Zaharias was a tomboy who excelled at many sports as a youngster and who went on to hold national, Olympic and world records in five different track and field events. During the Los Angeles Olympic Games in 1932 she won two gold medals and a silver medal, set a world record, and was the co-holder of two others.

During the mid-1930s, Zaharias turned her attention to golf and practised until her hands bled. She played in her first tournament in Texas in 1934 and a year later won the Texas Women's Amateur Championship. That same year, the United States Golf Association declared her a professional and banned her from amateur golf. Unable to make a living from the few tournaments open to her, she toured the country staging exhibition matches with professional golfer Gene Sarazen.

In 1940, Zaharias won the Texas Open and the Western Open golf tournaments. During the Second World War, she gave golf exhibitions to raise money for war bonds and agreed to abstain from professional athletics for three years in order to regain her amateur status, which was restored by the USGA in 1943.

After the war, she became one of the most successful golfers in history. During 1946 and 1947, she won 17 consecutive tournaments – including the British Women's Amateur Championship – a record that has never been equalled. A year later, Zaharias turned professional once again and went on to become the leading money winner on the women's professional circuit.

In the spring of 1953, doctors discovered that Zaharias had cancer, and she underwent surgery. She recovered to play in a golf tournament less than four months later. A year on, she won five tournaments, including the United States Women's Open. However, in 1955 the cancer returned, and she died in Galveston on 27 September 1956.

*Left:* An excellent all-round athlete, Babe Zaharias is widely regarded as the first high-profile woman golfer in the history of the sport.

*Left:* **Australia's Karrie Webb is widely regarded as the women's equivalent of Tiger Woods, such is her dominance on the LPGA Tour.**

## Nancy Lopez

Just as Arnold Palmer captivated the crowds and brought golf to a wider audience in the 1960s, so a young Mexican-American called Nancy Lopez set the women's game alight when she burst onto the scene as a teenager in the mid-1970s.

Lopez won her first golf tournament at the age of 12, turned professional at 20 and finished second in her first three tournaments. She went on to win five times in her first year – a record at the time – and followed up her impressive rookie year by winning nine times in 1978 and eight times in 1979.

By the time she reached 30, Lopez had racked up 35 Tour wins. In 1987 she became the youngest-ever player to be admitted into the Hall of Fame, but she had to wait for several months to receive her award as she had not been a professional for the requisite ten years.

Lopez married baseball star Ray Knight and tried hard to juggle her careers as a mother and as a golf professional. She won her 48th tournament in 1997 at the age of 40.

## Karrie Webb

Born in Queensland, Australia, in 1974, Karrie Webb started playing golf at the age of eight and represented her country in international competition six times between 1992 and 1994. She turned professional in 1994 and competed on the Futures Tour and the Women Professional Golfers' European Tour

(WPGET). She qualified for the LPGA Tour at her first attempt after finishing second at the Qualifying School, despite playing with a broken bone in her wrist.

During her 1996 rookie LPGA season, Webb captured four tournaments making her the second most successful rookie of all time behind Nancy Lopez. She also became the first rookie on either the LPGA or the men's PGA Tour to reach the $1 million mark in single season earnings.

Webb recorded a new career-low score of 63 during the third round of the 1997 Weetabix Women's British Open. She captured the 1997 Vare Trophy for lowest scoring average with 70.00, the lowest score in the award's 45-year history.

## Laura Davies

With her self-taught swing, laid-back and friendly manner and swashbuckling approach to the game, England's Laura Davies has been a crowd favourite since she burst onto the women's golf scene in the 1980s. Davies became one of the first European golfers to make an impact on the LPGA Tour in America and, in fact, she won her first major championship, the 1987 Women's US Open, before she had even joined the LPGA Tour.

A keen soccer and snooker fan and known for her regular visits to casinos, she has no less than 20 LPGA Tour victories to her name, including three Major Championships and has played in all six Solheim Cup encounters. In 1988, Davies was named a Member of the British Empire (MBE) by Queen Elizabeth II, and more recently was recognized by the LPGA as one of its top-50 players of all time.

## Annika Sorenstam

Annika Sorenstam was born in 1970, in Stockholm, and she enjoyed a highly successful amateur career. She was a member of the Swedish National Team from 1987 to 1992, was the World Amateur champion in 1992, runner-up at the 1992 US Women's Amateur Championship. In her time at the University of Arizona, she was the 1991 College Player of the Year, NCAA

Rolex Player of the Year award for the second time in three years. For the third consecutive year, she finished the season in the top-three on the season money list. In 1998, she again won Player of the Year (for the third time in four seasons), and she won the Vare Trophy for scoring average by becoming the first woman to break 70. Sorenstam was a member of the 1994, 1996 and 1998 Solheim Cup teams.

## Se Ri Pak

Se Ri Pak began playing golf at home in Korea when she was just 14 years old and she won 30 tournaments as an amateur in her home country before turning professional in 1996 at the age of just 19. After joining the paid ranks, Pak competed in 14 tournaments on the Korean LPGA Tour between 1996 and 1997, winning six of them and finishing runner-up seven times. After such amazing success on home soil, it came as no surprise when the shy 20-year-old announced that she was going to travel to America to attempt to qualify for the main LPGA Tour. It was also no surprise when she tied for first place in the Qualifying School and immediately secured her full Tour Card for the 1998 season.

The incredible Se Ri Pak success story continued when her first two victories on Tour in 1998 were Major Championships – The McDonald's LPGA Championship and the US Women's Open. Two further victories that year gave her four tournament wins in the season and, unsurprisingly, the Rolex Rookie of the Year award. Pak's Major Championship success in America has elevated her to superstar status at home in Korea, where she is one of the most famous people in the country and idolized by the public. Such is their level of expectation, however, that Pak has admitted to feeling the strain of carrying the burden of a nation's hopes on her shoulders and since her double major-winning success of 1998 it took her three years to add to her tally by winning the British Open at Sunningdale. Now it is only a matter of time before she wins at the highest level of the game more frequently.

champion in 1991 and runner-up the following year, 1992 PAC-10 champion and a 1991 and 1992 NCAA All-American.

Prior to joining the LPGA Tour in October 1993, Sorenstam competed on the WPG European Tour, where she was the 1993 Rookie of the Year. In 1994 on the LPGA Tour, Sorenstam, not surprisingly, was Rolex Rookie of the Year, becoming only the second foreign player to win the honour.

She is also the only player besides Nancy Lopez to have won Rolex Rookie of the Year and then Rolex Player of the Year and the Vare Trophy, which is awarded to the player with the lowest scoring average of the season, in successive years. In 1995, Sorenstam won the US Women's Open and successfully defended it the following year, shooting four rounds of par or better. In 1996, she won her second consecutive Vare Trophy with a season scoring average of 70.47. In 1997, she won the

# Professional Golf

## The Professional Tours

The women's professional Tours around the world have grown considerably in size and stature over the past decade. A 'Tour' is a series of professional competitions that moves from one venue to the next, week after week.

A tally is kept of each player's prize-money earned throughout the year, and a player's position on the money list determines their status as a tournament golfer and whether or not they retain the right to play on the Tour the following season. Those golfers who do not win enough money to automatically regain their card have to attend the Qualifying School to earn a chance of playing on Tour again.

In addition to the LPGA Tour in America, there are also Tours in Europe, Japan and Australia as well as many other countries throughout the world. Many golfers choose to spend a couple of years playing on the smaller and lesser-known Tours to learn the ropes, acclimatize to life away from home, hone their competitive skills and sharpen their game before heading to the main Tours where the prize money is greater.

## The Solheim Cup

Named after the late Karsten Solheim, the founder of the Karsten Manufacturing Corporation that makes Ping golf equipment, the Solheim Cup is the female equivalent of the Ryder Cup. Like the men's event, it is fiercely contested and is played every other year between Europe and America.

The first Solheim Cup match was played in 1990 at Lake Nona, in Florida, where the American team were convincing 11.5 to 4.5 winners. However, in 1992, at Dalmahoy, in Scotland, the European team came out on top with a five-point winning margin. The Americans won next and held the upper hand until Europe reclaimed the Cup, once again on Scottish soil, at Loch Lomond in 2000.

## THE MAJOR CHAMPIONSHIPS

### The Women's US Open

Almost as soon as the Women's Professional Golfers' Association was established in 1946, the US Women's Open became the premier tournament on the women's Tour. The Ladies' Professional Golfers' Association succeeded the WPGA in 1949 and conducted the tournament until 1952, after which the United States Golf Association took control.

The Open was originally a matchplay tournament in its first year, but since 1947, it has been run as a 72-hole strokeplay event. If two or more golfers are tied after 72 holes, they meet in an 18-hole playoff.

### The Nabisco Tournament

American singer and television hostess Dina Shore inaugurated this LPGA Tour event in 1972 and the tournament was known as the Colgate Dinah Shore Tournament until 1982 when Nabisco took over the sponsorship. The event gained its Major Championship status in 1983. Now known simply as the Nabisco Tournament, the winner still receives the Dinah Shore Trophy.

### The McDonald's Championship

The LPGA Championship was launched in 1955 at Orchard Ridge GC, in Indiana, as a 54-hole strokeplay event. The following year, the bold step was taken to increase the championship to a 72-hole event at a time when most women's events were 54 holes. The event has produced some top quality winners, including Mickey Wright, Nancy Lopez, Laura Davies and Karrie Webb.

### The British Open

Unlike the men's game, where the British Open is the oldest and generally regarded as the most prestigious of the Majors, The Women's British Open is the newcomer to the Grand Slam events. It was only awarded Major Championship status in 2001, when it replaced the Du Maurier Classic. The championship is played on a rota of impressive and traditional British courses, including Sunningdale, Royal Birkdale and Royal Lytham & St Annes.

# *Swing Basics*

**A**sk any top golfer to offer one piece of advice to a beginner, and invariably they will say: 'Work on the fundamentals of the game right from the outset.' The grip, posture and clubface alignment are not the most interesting topics to discuss, but they are undoubtedly the most important. If you do not hold the club properly, aim carefully and stand to the ball correctly, your swing will be a shambles. At worst, you will struggle to make a good contact with the ball. At best, your swing will be riddled with compensations to counteract your sloppy basics, all of which will eat away at your power and accuracy.

The world's top golfers are meticulous about the way in which they hold the club, stand to the ball and aim the clubface and their body. They know that if they encounter a swing problem on the course, most of the time it can be traced back to an anomaly at address. The moral of the story is that you will maximize your chances of making a good swing if you eradicate errors at the set-up stage.

# How to form the correct grip

When you visit your local golf course you will see all kinds of weird and wonderful variations of bad golf grips, but very few good ones. Golfers seem to be able to contort their hands into all sorts of strange positions on the club, but an effective and orthodox grip is easier to form than you think. All you need is a little know-how and a good measure of perseverance.

The grip is one of golf's great enigmas; and instructional books and videos have devoted many words to the subject. However, all too often the message must get confused along the line, because most amateur golfers still hold the club incorrectly. The first thing that you should understand is that your grip should complement the natural shape of your forearms and not contort you into an uncomfortable position. Regularly practise the step-by-step procedure illustrated below until it becomes an instinctive and almost involuntary act. You should also continually check the positions of your hands and forearms on the club, as this will help to ensure that bad habits do not creep into your game unnoticed.

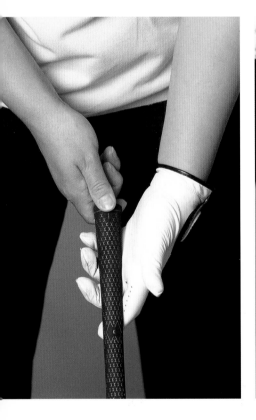

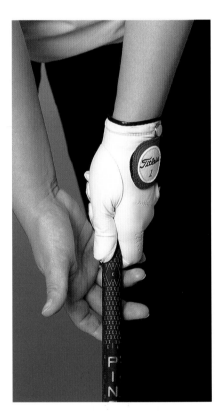

**1** Allow your left arm to hang naturally by your side and then curl the fingers of your left hand around the handle of the club. Rest the grip at the base of the fingers.

**2** Your left thumb should be positioned just right of centre on the grip pointing straight down. To achieve this position without twisting your forearm to the left, you will need to create a slight angle at the base of your wrist.

**3** The same grip principles used to place the left hand apply when positioning the right hand. Allow the club to rest at the base of the fingers, but do not allow your right forearm to twist out of position as you take hold of the club.

## Grip Pointers

- Forearms should remain in a neutral position as you place your hands on the grip
- Hold the club more in the hands than the palms for power and control
- A similar number of knuckles should be visible on both hands

## THE GRIP

### 'Neutral' forearms form the foundation

**1** Your grip should be as natural as possible. If you stand with your arms hanging by your sides, you will notice that your forearms turn inwards so that the palms of your hands face your thighs.

**2** Now if you hold your arms out in front of you and bring your hands together, this is what your hands should look like when they are placed together on the golf club. There should be a slight angle at the base of both wrists and two to three knuckles showing on each hand.

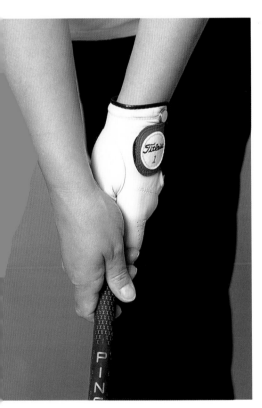

**4** Always ensure that you can see more of the back of your hand than the palm when placing it on the grip. Ideally, you should see a similar number of knuckles on each hand as you look down at your completed grip.

# Overlap or interlock?

You have several different options when it comes to linking your two hands together on the grip. A small minority of golfers hold the club in a 'baseball-style', where their hands do not link together at all but instead are positioned close together on the grip. Many players claim that this way of holding the club allows them to generate more power. However, most coaches advocate that the hands should be linked together and most of the top players prefer this method because of its solid feel. The two most popular techniques used to link the hands together are the overlapping and the interlocking grips. The overlapping grip, where the little finger on the right hand overlaps the left hand and rests in the ridge between the index and second finger, is most common.

A variation on the theme is the interlocking grip, where the little finger on the right hand slots in between the base of the index and second finger on the left hand, rather than resting on top.

Women with small hands may prefer the interlocking grip as it provides a more secure hold over the club. Tiger Woods and Jack Nicklaus both hold the club in this way, so you will be in good company if you opt for this variation.

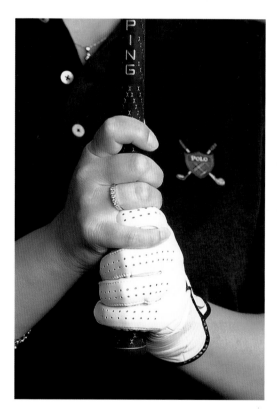

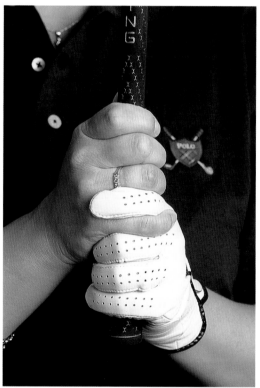

**1** To form an overlapping grip, place your hands on the club in a baseball-style and then slot the little finger on your right hand onto the ridge created between your left index finger and your second finger.

**2** To form an interlocking grip, once again place your hands on the club in a baseball-style and then simply allow the little finger on your right hand to interlock with your left index finger

## Grip Pointers

● Never jam your hands tightly together when linking them on the grip
● Players with small hands may find that the interlocking grip gives them more control
● Avoid gripping the club too tightly as this will create tension in your hands, forearms and shoulders

## EQUIPMENT TIP

### Match your grips to your hands

Many women have small hands and while this is not necessarily a problem, you must be careful when choosing the size and types of grip you have fitted on your clubs. Grips that are too thick will stop your wrists from hinging effectively during the swing and will prevent you from releasing the club powerfully through impact. Grips that are too thin will encourage too much 'loose' hand action in the swing. Ideally, your fingertips should just reach the pad of flesh at the base of your thumb when you hold the club.

## FEEL THE WEIGHT OF THE CLUBHEAD

Whichever method of grip you choose, your hands should work together as a single unit. The overall feel should be soft and light. Avoid squeezing the club too tightly, as tension in the hands quickly spreads up the forearms into the shoulders and the rest of the body. Your grip should be light enough to sense the weight of the clubhead in your hands, and it should allow you to 'waggle' the club around freely and quickly.

# How a bad grip affects your game

*Left:* **A good grip allows the rest of your swing to slot neatly into place. A bad grip can have a devastating effect on your swing and your scores.**

product of ingrained habits, and as such they usually feel very comfortable to the golfer concerned. If that is the case with you, any alterations that you make to the way in which you hold the club will feel totally unnatural and awkward for quite a while. Some of the short-term side effects of changing your grip include a loss of confidence, tempo and timing, the end results of which can be very disheartening. Although it will be tempting to revert back to your old grip if you are constantly hitting the ball sideways or struggling to get the ball airborne, you should resist the temptation to slip back to your old ways and instead play through this frustrating period because your game will benefit in the long run.

## Getting used to your grip

A good way to accelerate the familiarization process with your new grip is to constantly practise gripping and re-gripping the club. You do not necessarily have to do this in a golf environment either. As long as you have a golf club to hand you can work on your grip literally anywhere – watching the television at home, in your lunch-break at the office or any time you have a few spare moments to yourself. Building a new grip is all about destroying your old bad habits and creating new effective ones, so the more you practise the quicker the changes will blend into your game.

Once you have developed an orthodox grip, most of the hard work is done, but you should never get too complacent since bad habits can easily come back to haunt you. The world's top players constantly review the way in which they grip the club and stand to the ball, and you should be just as diligent because it does not take long for a small flaw to escalate into a big problem if left unchecked. Always remember that if you take care of the basics, the swing will look after itself.

As any self-respecting golf professional will gladly tell you, a poor grip can have a devastating effect upon your swing, but thankfully it is usually a relatively straightforward problem to overcome. On the opposite page we have highlighted the two most common mistakes, together with the detrimental results they have upon your address position and, in turn, the whole of your game. Compare the photographs on the right with your own grip and set-up. If they look at all similar, head to your nearest golf professional for emergency treatment.

One very important point to remember about changing your grip, however, is that it can often take a while to reap the rewards of your hard work. Bad grips are nearly always the

## WEAK GRIP AIMS FOREARMS AND BODY LEFT OF TARGET

### Weak grip – right hand and forearm dominate

If your hands look something like this, where the right hand is positioned too much on top of the club and the left hand too far underneath, you have what is known as a 'weak' grip. This usually manifests itself in the form of sliced shots to the right or pulls to the left.

A weak grip normally causes your right shoulder to dominate the address position and your upper body and forearms to aim left of the target line. From here, it is extremely difficult to avoid swinging the club outside the correct path at too steep an angle on the backswing.

## STRONG GRIP AIMS FOREARMS AND BODY RIGHT OF TARGET

### Strong grip – left forearm and hand dominate

If your hands look something like this, where your left hand is positioned too much on top of the club with the right hand forced underneath, you have what is known as a 'strong' grip. This can lead to badly hooked shots to the left or pushed shots out to the right. The effect of a strong grip is that it forces your left shoulder to rise too much at address. Your upper body and forearms aim well right of the target, leading you to swing the club on an exaggerated path inside the target line.

# Learning how to aim the club and your body correctly

If the grip is the most badly abused of all the swing fundamentals, then alignment is probably the most neglected – by players of all levels. To hit consistently straight shots, the clubface must be not only aimed at your target correctly, but also aligned squarely to your body. If the clubface and your feet, hips and shoulders are at odds with each other, you will struggle to swing the club on the correct path, making it difficult to strike the ball powerfully and accurately.

The first misconception about alignment is that you should aim your body at the target. This advice, however, ignores the fact that you actually stand a couple of feet away from the ball and the clubface at address. Therefore, if both the clubface and your body are aiming at the target, your shoulders will actually be aiming too far to the right.

In a good golf swing, the clubface and body are aligned squarely to each other. The clubface aims directly at the target, while the rest of your body aims parallel to, but left of, the target. To help you understand and remember the principles of good alignment, visualize yourself standing on a railway line as you hit a shot. The clubface, ball and the target will all be on the outer rail, while your feet and shoulders will all be on the inner rail. The two lines never meet.

## Shoulder alignment

After aiming the clubface carefully, the next key area of the alignment process is the positioning of your shoulders. Many amateurs concentrate more on where their feet are aiming, but although it is advisable to have your feet positioned square to the target, you do not hit the ball with your feet. It is the position of your shoulders that dictates the line of the swing path, so it is vital that your upper body is aligned correctly.

The majority of the world's top players constantly monitor their alignment because, along with the rest of the set-up, it is very difficult to see where the clubface and the body are aiming when you are standing right on top of the ball. For this very reason, you will often see the professionals lay a club on the ground parallel to their target line as a reference point for their alignment routine. This enables them to aim the clubface and position their feet and shoulders correctly prior to every single practice shot they hit. It also serves to groove the feelings associated with the correct alignment position so that there is less chance that things will go wrong when it comes to hitting shots on the golf course itself.

*Left:* It is advisable to get into the habit of practising with a club laid on the ground to help you with your alignment routine.

## Good alignment takes its lead from the clubface

Golfers of all levels struggle with their alignment for the simple reason that when you hit the ball, you are standing side on to a target that is up to 200yds away in the distance. Poor alignment is a very common set-up flaw.

Many golfers make the mistake of setting-up over the ball before even thinking about aiming their body and the clubface. However, such an approach is a recipe for disaster. Good alignment takes its lead from the clubface. Make sure

that you start your address routine by carefully aiming the clubface at your intended target. Once you have done that, you then have a reference point from which you can aim your body – feet, hips and shoulders – squarely to that initial line.

A good way to groove this routine on the driving range is to place two clubs on the ground parallel to each other as guides. After hitting several shots with the clubs in place you will soon develop an instinctive awareness for the correct target line and this will prove invaluable when out on the course for real.

**1** Aiming the clubface at your intended target should be the first step of your address routine. Always aim the clubface before you position your feet and shoulders at address.

**2** Constantly refer to the target as you aim the clubface and position your upper body. Check and double-check that the clubface is aiming where you want the ball to go.

**3** The last step of the routine is to position your feet. Stick to this routine on every shot you play – even chips and putts – to ensure that you have lined up correctly each time.

# Posture: preparing for power

Golf is an athletic sport that places great demands upon the player. An aspiring golfer requires strength, flexibility and hand-eye coordination to hit the ball well. Just as you would not expect a tennis player to slouch as she was preparing to serve, so a golfer's set-up must reflect the energy, effort and purpose that she is going to put into her swing.

Your posture should look and feel dynamic. Posture is vital because golf is in many respects an angular sport. For maximum consistency, the angles you create with your back, upper body and legs must be maintained throughout the swing. Most notably, creating and then maintaining a good spine angle is fundamental to your ability to make a good turn and remain in balance as you swing back and through.

*Left:* **In order to hit the ball powerfully and accurately, you must stand to the ball in an athletic and comfortable manner.**

**1** The most common posture flaw among women golfers is slouching with the upper body, sitting too far back on the heels and jamming the chin against the chest.

**2** The result of the poor posture is that the shoulders are forced to tilt instead of turn and the player has to lift her arms straight up into the air to make a swing.

**1** A good posture enables you to create a good spine angle that you can rotate your upper body around and allows your arms to hang naturally almost straight down from your shoulders.

The key to creating a good posture is tilting forwards from your hips to reach the ball. Many women make the mistake of simply bending their legs and lowering their bottom. However, this does not place you in a balanced and powerful position.

## The effects of poor posture

As you have probably realized, a good golf swing is a chain reaction. Start the swing well and there is every chance that the rest will slot neatly into place. Start poorly, however, and things generally deteriorate.

Posture is a problem area for many women golfers. The most common example is where the shoulders are slumped, the bottom is tucked in and the weight set too far back on the heels. From this unstable and weak address position, it is difficult to generate any real power and consistency. Because the shoulders cannot turn correctly, the golfer is forced into lifting her arms to make a backswing. The result is that the arms collapse at the top of the swing and from that point on, the quality of the shot is unpredictable.

The correct set-up has a number of significant differences. Notice how the spine is angled more over the ball, how the bottom sticks out a little to counterbalance it and how the arms now hang much more freely from the shoulders, rather like a pendulum. The weight is also set more towards the balls of the feet, which allows the golfer to turn without fear of falling backwards and losing balance. From this more athletic-looking set-up, the golfer can swing her arms and her body into a powerful position at the top of the backswing.

**2** The athletic posture permits an effective shoulder turn, allows the weight to transfer onto your right during the backswing and maximizes your chances of a controlled, powerful swing.

## DIFFERENT CLUB DIFFERENT POSTURE

Each golf club has a different length shaft, so you will need to adjust your posture according to the club you are using. For example, you must stand closer to the ball when hitting your pitching wedge, which is one of your shortest clubs, than when hitting your driver, which is the longest club in your bag.

Your posture should feel similar with each club, although your spine angle will naturally be more upright when hitting a longer club. When using shorter clubs you will need to tilt your upper body further forward so that you can reach the ball.

# *Pre-shot routine*

The best way to address the ball consistently is to incorporate the key elements of the set-up – the grip, aim, posture and stance – into a well-grooved routine. An effective set-up routine relies on a mental checklist that can be recalled prior to playing every shot, and it is likely to be as individual as a player's fingerprints. Nevertheless, the most effective routines contain several key elements (highlighted below), which can be used as a starting point.

In addition to keeping your swing basics in check, a pre-shot routine also helps you perform better under pressure, as it grooves muscle memory and allows you to slip into auto-pilot as you prepare to play an important shot.

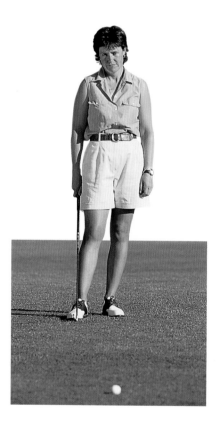  

**1** Visualize the shot. Stand several feet behind the ball and picture the shot you want to hit. If you do not know what you are trying to achieve, you have little chance of executing an effective shot.

**2** It is easier to line up to a target that is just a few feet away than one that is 150yds in the distance, so pick out an intermediate target a few feet in front of your ball. A stone, a divot, a leaf or an old tee are ideal.

**3** Aim the clubface carefully at the target before you position your feet and shoulders. It is crucial to get this part of the routine right, as your body will take its lead from the clubface alignment.

## Routine Pointers

- Start routine by visualizing the shot you want to hit
- Use your routine to slot into the correct address position each and every time
- A well-grooved routine will help you play better under pressure

**4** Complete your routine by positioning your feet and shoulders. You can now go ahead and make a free-flowing swing with confidence.

## STANCE AND BALL POSITION

The width of your stance is a matter of preference. However, there are a few ground rules. Firstly, as the length of the club increases your stance widens to create the extra stability needed to cope with the increase in swing speed. When hitting a driver your stance should be at its widest, while your wedges require your feet to be closer together.

Your feet should be just over shoulder-width apart for the driver. The stance narrows progressively down through the bag until you reach a point where your stance is just less than the width of your shoulders for a full shot with a sand wedge.

Ball position is another area of personal preference. Coaches are divided into two schools of thought. The first says that the ball should be played a couple of inches inside the left heel for every club, while the right foot changes position to either widen or narrow the stance. The more popular view, however, is that ball position should vary according to the club. Starting with a ball position just inside the left heel for the driver, the ball moves progressively back until it is played directly in the centre of the feet. The theory is that positioning the ball further forward enables you to make a sweeping swing with the woods, while playing the ball further back allows you to create the steeper descending blow that is required when hitting an iron.

Whichever method you choose, make sure that the rest of your fundamentals are solid. A little experimentation will determine which option works best for you.

# Faults and fixes

As mentioned on the previous pages, a good posture is one of the key fundamentals of your game since the angles that you create at address will dictate the plane of your swing, your swing path, the amount of controlled power you can generate and, in turn, the quality of your ball-striking. To hit the ball powerfully and consistently, you need a solid and athletic base upon which you can turn your upper body freely back and through around a distinctive spine angle.

## Problems of poor posture

Despite its obvious importance, poor posture is probably the most common swing fault found among higher handicap women golfers and beginners. The main problem appears to stem from a reluctance to create 'sharp' angles with the upper and lower body at address. Instead of tilting forwards from the hips to lower the clubhead to the ball while keeping the lower part of the spine fairly straight, many women simply bend their knees and allow their weight to fall back on their heels. From this 'soft' and weak address position it is almost impossible to generate any worthwhile power. Because your spine angle is too 'soft' and curved, your upper body does not have an axis around which it can coil, while setting up with too much weight on the heels makes it extremely difficult to turn the shoulders without losing your balance.

The normal consequence of this combination of errors and poor positions is that the golfer is forced into simply lifting her arms straight up into the air to make a backswing. However, because the shoulders cannot turn correctly, the player's weight often remains on the front foot during the backswing, causing the shoulders to tilt instead. When this occurs the list of bad shots is virtually endless as numerous compensations are required to return the clubface to the ball squarely and powerfully. Not surprisingly, most amateurs struggle to save the shot. If you can focus on positioning your body correctly at address you stand a very good chance of making a decent swing, as you give each area of the swing an opportunity to move as it should do.

## POSTURE REMINDERS

❶ Always bend forward from the hips to lower yourself and the clubhead to the ball.

❷ Allow your bottom to stick out a little to counterbalance the angle created by tilting forwards.

❸ Keep your lower back as straight as possible so that your upper body can coil around it more easily.

❹ Lightly flex your knees to remove the tension from your legs but without losing any height.

## FAULT

### • The classic 'S'-shaped posture

This is probably the most common posture flaw among women golfers. Instead of creating sharp angles with her lower back, bottom and legs, the golfer here has simply lowered her whole body to reach the ball. The end result is that her spine angle is curved, her bottom is tucked in and most of her weight is set towards her heels. This position is known as the 'S'-shaped posture because of the rounded curves created by the upper and lower body. It is a combination that makes it virtually impossible to turn the shoulders correctly.

You can also tell that it will be very difficult for the player to make a powerful swing from this position. The golfer looks out of balance and cramped at address.

## FIX

### Extend the club in front of you, tilt from the hips

A good posture exercise is to stand upright with your arms gently outstretched, holding the club horizontal to the ground. Now tilt forwards from your hips, not your waist, to lower the club to the ground. Keep your spine angle straight and allow your bottom to stick out a little as you move.

Gently flex your knees so that you remove the tension from your legs but do not lose height. This creates a much better spine angle, the arms hang more naturally and there is more room underneath the chin to turn the upper body correctly.

## FIX

### Tilt forward from the hips to lower the club to the ground

Another excellent practice exercise to help you feel how you should tilt forwards from your hips to lower yourself to the ball is to stand upright holding a club across the top of your thighs.

Now gently push the club into your body as you tilt forwards while keeping your spine angle nice and straight. This will give you the feeling of how your upper body should be angled more over the ball at the address position.

# *The Golf Swing*

The fact that more books have been written about the golf swing than any other aspect of sporting technique should give you some idea of how frustrating golf is for many people. However, the main reason why many golfers continually struggle with their game is that they are too impatient to learn the basics and, therefore, stand to the ball poorly from day one. Without a good grip, posture and alignment, you will never be able to swing like Annika Sorenstam, no matter how talented you are.

In this chapter, we will look at the key positions in the swing, but first, a few words of caution. Although the photos on the following pages have captured the swing at various key positions, it is important to remember that in reality the swing is one continuous motion. While it is advisable to develop a swing that is technically correct, it should not come at the expense of good rhythm and motion. It is impossible to try to swing the club through six or seven checkpoints, but one or two will help focus your mind. For the most part, complex swing thoughts are best left on the practice ground. On the golf course, your greatest ally is good rhythm.

# *Learn to turn your shoulders*

The foundation of any good golf swing is a solid coil. In the swing, your upper body should rotate around the spine angle that you create with your lower back at address to create power and control the speed and tempo of your swing.

Turning your upper body back and through allows your weight to move onto your right side during the backswing and then onto the front foot in the downswing as you swing the clubhead back down to the ball and towards the target. If your shoulders tilt instead of turn, it is difficult to transfer your weight onto the front foot correctly and your shots will lack power and consistency. The exercise below will help you to experience the correct coiling motion.

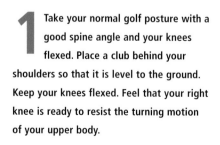

**1** Take your normal golf posture with a good spine angle and your knees flexed. Place a club behind your shoulders so that it is level to the ground. Keep your knees flexed. Feel that your right knee is ready to resist the turning motion of your upper body.

**2** Coil your upper body around the angle of your spine. If you have done this correctly, the left end of the club should have moved downwards slightly. This is because your spine is not vertical during the swing but angled forwards slightly. You should also feel some tension in your right knee as it resists the coil while your weight transfers onto your right side.

**3** To simulate the downswing, simply coil your shoulders around your spine angle until the club points toward the target. Allow your weight to move onto your front foot. As you turn through to a full finish it is acceptable for your spine angle and your left leg to straighten once you have struck the ball.

## Swing Pointers

- **Upper body coils around the axis of the spine**
- **Right knee resists the coiling motion of the upper body**
- **Maintain the flex in your right knee and your spine angle during the backswing**
- **Shoulders will not turn horizontally because spine is angled downwards at address**

# Arms swing as shoulders turn

Once you have trained your upper body to coil correctly in the swing, adding the arms and the hands to the swing is fairly straightforward. As your body turns back and through during the swing, you swing your arms up and down.

It sounds simple enough, but the key point to note is that the two movements must be synchronized. If your shoulders turn faster than you swing your arms, you will run into problems with your timing and tempo and probably end up swinging your arms too far behind you on a flat swing plane, which will cause problems with your ball striking. Similarly, if your arms swing upwards quickly but your shoulders turn slowly, your backswing is likely to become too steep and once again you will encounter problems with your timing, tempo and ball striking. Only when the swinging motion of your arms matches the turning of your shoulders is power maximized.

# Wrists hinge to create power

In any sport where the hands are used to hit a ball, such as tennis, baseball or squash, the wrists play a key role in creating and applying power to the shot. Golf is no different. If your grip is correctly formed and you are not holding the club excessively tightly, you should find that your wrists will hinge automatically in your backswing in response to the swinging motion of your arms and the weight of the clubhead. This wrist action is vital since it sets the club on the correct swing plane and applies power to the ball through impact. If your swing contains little or no wrist hinge, you will swing the club too much around yourself and not generate enough power.

## SWING KEYS

❶ Maintain your spine angle throughout the swing until you have struck the ball.

❷ Keep your right knee flexed during the backswing and do not allow your weight to move onto the outside of your right foot.

❸ As your upper body turns, swing your arms up and away from the ball.

❹ Allow your wrists to hinge 90 degrees on the backswing.

❺ Maintain your height throughout the whole swing for consistent ball striking.

*Left:* Maintaining the flex in your right knee enables you to maintain your height and forces your arms to swing upwards rather than around your body.

The right knee must retain its flex and resist the coil of your upper body during the backswing for the following four reasons:

*To help maintain your height during the swing.*

If the right knee remains flexed, your height remains consistent and you maximize your chances of striking the ball cleanly.

*To force your upper body to turn rather than sway laterally to the right.*

Although it may feel powerful, if you allow your upper body to sway laterally across to the right in your backswing, you will obviously have to slide back across to the left in the downswing by exactly the same amount in order to strike the ball correctly. While you can get away with this if your timing is good, it inevitably leads to inconsistencies in the long run.

*To help the arms swing upwards instead of around the body.*

When your right knee resists the coiling motion of your upper body, your arms are forced to swing upwards rather than around your body, leading to a more effective swing plane and swing path.

*To encourage a full wrist hinge*

For the same reasons that encourage the arms to swing upwards, the wrists are forced to hinge the club upwards rather than allowing it to swing around the body.

## The right knee is your anchor

The importance of maintaining the flex and resistance in the right knee during the backswing cannot be overstated. While the coiling motion of your upper body is the dynamo of the swing, the right knee is the chassis that holds everything in place. It is the anchor of your swing.

For reasons normally associated with problems that have occurred at the address position and, in particular, from poor posture, many women allow their right leg to straighten in the backswing. When this occurs, there are a number of disastrous knock-on effects. Firstly, you normally lose your spine angle, which prevents your shoulders from turning correctly. The usual consequence of this is that your shoulders end up tilting instead, causing your backswing to become too steep and your weight to remain stuck on your front foot.

The other side effect is that straightening the right knee actually changes your height during the backswing. If this happens you will obviously have to compensate at some later stage in the swing to return the clubface squarely and powerfully to the back of the ball without mishitting it.

---

## QUICK TIP

### How to feel the perfect blend of wrists, arms and shoulders

While you are learning the swing, it can be confusing to work on swinging your arms, coiling your shoulders and hinging your wrists at the same time. A good exercise to help you experience what the correct blend should feel like is to address the ball normally, then hinge your wrists upwards in front of you without moving your hands up in the air. Now turn your shoulders around your spine angle to experience the perfect backswing position.

### Backswing Pointers

- Swing your arms upwards in the backswing rather than around your body
- Allow your wrists to hinge naturally and fully
- Retain flex and resistance in right knee so that arms swing upwards and wrists hinge
- Your wrists release the club through impact and re-hinge in follow-through

## Hit balls with legs crossed to feel your arms swing correctly

Although you can perform this exercise to help you focus on your arm swing and wrist action, this is also a good all-round drill to improve virtually every aspect of your swing. By crossing your legs as you hit the ball, you remove some of your stability and are automatically forced to swing the club more rhythmically. This is a particularly effective exercise since it forces your arms to swing along the correct path, and it also encourages a full hinge of the wrists. It will liven up a lazy hand action through impact, since you are forced to release the clubhead freely to send it forwards in the air.

**1** Stand to the ball normally, cross your legs at address. This forces your arms to swing upwards and your wrists to hinge actively on the backswing.

**2** Maintaining your rhythm, swing your arms back down to the ball in a controlled manner, noticing how your forearms and hands release the club.

**3** Keeping your legs crossed in the downswing will force your arms to swing up and through as your wrists hinge the club upwards again.

## Address: set-up determines swing

**1** An excellent example of good posture where the arms hang almost vertically from the shoulders. The knees are lightly flexed and the upper body is angled forwards towards the ball.

**2** The stance is approximately shoulder-width apart, the ball is just forward of centre between the feet and the hands are just ahead of the ball. Note that the right shoulder is set a little below the left as a result of the right hand being placed lower than the left on the grip. The left arm and the clubshaft form virtually a straight line, which will apply maximum pressure to the ball at impact.

## The takeaway

**1** The arms and shoulders move the club away together. The clubface remains outside of the hands, and if you drew a line through the shaft of the club it would point straight at the ball.

**2** Already you can see how the weight is beginning to move onto the right side as the arms swing the club away. The shoulders have yet to begin to turn, although it is clear that the right knee and hip are remaining fixed in position and not sliding laterally to the right as the weight moves onto the right side. The hands and the clubhead are still nice and low.

## Halfway back

**1** The right knee has retained its flex and the spine angle remains the same, too. As the shoulders have coiled, the arms have swung upwards, helped by a hinging of the wrists.

**2** Halfway back, the right knee and hip have barely changed position from the last frame. The left arm remains extended to create width and power and the wrists have hinged the club upwards from the position in the previous photograph. The head remains centred over the ball and the left arm and the clubshaft to create a 90-degree angle by the time the left arm is horizontal to the ground.

## The top of the backswing

**1** The right knee remains flexed, the spine angle has not shifted position and the clubshaft is aiming square to the target line at the top of the backswing.

**2** The shoulders have completed a full turn, the left arm is extended but not dead straight and the hands are above head height. The right knee and hip have resisted the coiling motion perfectly and there is no sign of any kind of lateral sway or movement. The upper body has coiled against the resistance of the lower body and almost all of the weight is on the inside of the right foot.

## Starting down: keep the transition smooth

**1** As the left knee and hip initiate the downswing, the hands and arms automatically drop down. Note how the left arm remains extended and how the left hip is beginning to clear out of the way.

**2** The weight is rapidly transferring across to the front foot to provide momentum to the shot. The wrist hinge created in the backswing has been maintained ready for release through impact. Once again, however, there is no hint of any sliding with the lower body. The leg action is solid and understated, yet the position oozes a sense of controlled power ready for the next important stage.

## Impact: the moment of truth

**1** Most powerful hitters have the majority of their weight on the front foot at the point of impact. The left hip has cleared out of the way, giving the arms and shoulders room to fire through.

**2** Just as the left arm and the clubshaft formed a straight line at address, so they do again at impact to apply maximum power and leverage to the ball. See how the head has remained steady, still positioned behind the ball – a sure sign that the power has been delivered in a controlled manner rather than via a lunge at the ball with the upper body. All the weight is on the front foot now.

## The release: fire the forearms through the ball

**1** Remember what I said earlier about hitting the ball hard? Here is a fine example of how the right side has fired aggressively through impact. The spine angle still remains the same as at address.

**2** Extension through impact is a key to power and accuracy. Note how the right shoulder has fired through under the chin and how the right arm remains fully extended. The right forearm has rotated to powerfully release the clubface through impact. The weight is clearly moving forwards toward the target, and the left hip is still clearing rapidly out of the way.

## The finish: show a clean set of spikes

**1** Even in the finish position, the spine angle created at address has been maintained. The right knee has kicked in towards the target and you can see every single spike on the right shoe.

**2** Standing tall and proud at the finish, all of the weight is now on the front foot and if the player lifted her right toe off the ground she would remain standing. A tell-tale sign of a powerful swing is when the right shoulder points towards the target. The hands are held nice and high, and a line drawn vertically down from the right shoulder would pass through the right hip, the left knee and the left foot.

# *Faults and fixes*

## *FAULT*

### • *The reverse pivot*

The reverse pivot keeps golf professionals in business throughout the year. It is by far the most common fault among golfers of all ages and sexes. As the name suggests, rather than pivoting correctly to turn and allow the weight to transfer across to the right side during the backswing, the upper body tilts instead and the exact opposite happens. The weight falls onto the front foot on the backswing and then onto the back foot in the downswing. If your weight is moving backwards while you are trying to hit the ball forwards, you inevitably struggle to find power and consistency. It is difficult to characterize the type of bad shots that are associated with this particular fault because virtually anything can happen – including the occasional fantastically struck effort – but far more often than not the results are disappointing.

## *FIX*

### • *Lift left foot off the ground to test your weight transference*

An excellent way to find out if you have a reverse pivot is to make your backswing then lift your left foot off the ground. If you cannot do this, or if you struggle to do so without losing your balance, you are tilting your shoulders rather than turning them.

As you make your swing, focus on keeping your right knee flexed as you allow your weight to transfer across onto your right side. Make plenty of practice swings focusing on this feeling and finish each one by raising your left foot off the ground.

## *FAULT*

### • *Allowing the right leg to straighten*

As mentioned earlier in this book, holding the flex in your right knee plays a crucial role in the swing. It ensures that you retain your height and also harnesses the power that you create when you coil your shoulders. If you allow the right knee to straighten, your upper body straightens too, your weight normally gets stuck on your front foot and you fail to complete your backswing correctly. Needless to say, the consequences are generally unimpressive.

This particular swing flaw will often cause, or occur as a result of, the reverse pivot highlighted on the opposite page. So if you can eradicate this flaw from your game, the chances are the reverse pivot will disappear, too.

## *FIX*

### • *Place a ball under your right heel*

An instant fix to stop your right knee straightening is to place a ball under your right heel when you hit practice shots. You are forced into keeping your right knee flexed as straightening it will cause you to stamp the ball into the ground.

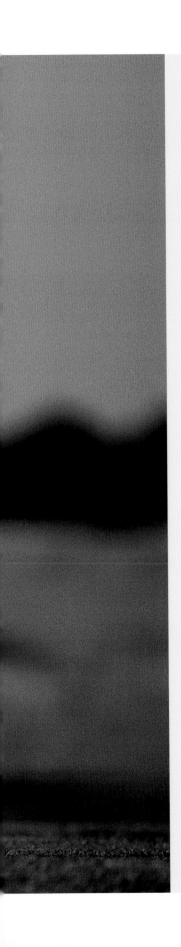

# *The Long Game*

**M**any people argue that the short game and putting are the two keys to good scoring. Do not believe a word of it. While a great touch around the green and a silky smooth putting stroke will undoubtedly bail you out of trouble from time to time they are, by and large, recovery shots. It stands to reason that if you improve your long game, you will not need to scramble so much for your pars, and the putts you face will be more likely to be for birdies.

However, if you still need convincing, look at the top players on the Ladies' Tour: Karrie Webb, Se Ri Pak and Annika Sorenstam are all powerful hitters. Great chippers and putters, certainly, but it is no coincidence that these same players, in addition to being near the top of the Money List, all rank highly in the 'driving accuracy' and 'greens hit in regulation' statistics recorded by the LPGA Tour. So if you want to make a real difference to your scores, take time to brush up on your long game.

# Driving

## Set up for a sweeping success

The driver is designed to make contact with the ball ever so slightly on the upswing. The clubhead sweeps it forwards and upwards off of the tee. To encourage a shallower, sweeping motion through impact, play the ball well forward in your stance, virtually opposite your left instep. Place extra weight on your right side at address so that your head is a few inches behind the ball. Your left shoulder and hip should feel a little higher than the right and, as a result, your spine should be angled slightly away from the target, instead of being vertical.

Another important aspect of the driver address position is to set up with the left arm and the shaft of the club forming a straight line. This encourages a wide, sweeping takeaway and creates power through impact. If they are out of line they cannot apply as much power and pressure to the ball.

**1** Once you have set up to the ball correctly, the driver swing is no different to any other shot. Start your swing extra smoothly. Sweep the clubhead away low to the ground for the first few feet of the backswing and feel your weight settle onto your right side.

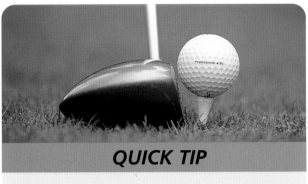

## Driving lessons

Recent research has revealed that the average golfer would improve her score by about four or five shots if a top professional, such as Sweden's Annika Sorenstam, did all the putting for her on an 18-hole round. However, the very same golfer would improve by about 12 shots per round if Sorenstam hit every single tee shot for her instead. The statistics, on this occasion, do not lie and prove how important good driving is to your overall score.

Many women golfers who lack confidence with a driver, attempt to steer the ball down the fairway with a tentative and gentle swing. Unfortunately, that strategy rarely works. You have to swing the driver confidently and authoritatively. If you watch the top players off the tee, you will notice that every one, without exception, commits fully to the shot.

### QUICK TIP

### Set the logo level with the clubhead

Many players are unsure how high to tee the ball and, although it sounds trivial, the incorrect tee height can adversely affect your drives. If the ball is teed too low, you have to hit down steeply, while if it is too high, your swing can become too flat as you try to avoid skied and mishit drives. A good reference is to tee up with the logo of the ball level with the top of the clubhead.

**2** At the top of your backswing, the clubshaft should be parallel to the ground and your right knee should maintain the flex and resistance introduced at the address position. Turn your shoulders through 90 degrees so that your back faces the target.

**3** Lunging at the ball for power rarely has the desired effect. Allow your weight to move gently onto the left side and swing your arms back down to the ball in front of your body. This action will help you sweep the ball off the tee. Keep your head behind the ball at impact.

**4** The length of the club and the momentum of the swing will pull you into a position where your right shoulder is nearest to the target at the finish. By now, most of your weight will be on your front foot and your chest will be facing to the left of the target.

# Fairway woods and long irons

## Fairway woods

When using fairway woods the same principles apply as for driving, with the exception that the ball is no longer placed on a tee peg. You still require the shallow approach into the ball and the sweeping attack that will catch the ball ever so slightly on the upswing.

On the golf course, address the ball with your weight fairly evenly distributed or, if anything, with just a little extra weight on your right side. As with the driver, your right shoulder and hip should be set lower than the left. Women tend to be very good fairway-wood players, as their smooth rhythm and tempo suit the playing characteristics of the club. Once again allow your weight to settle into your right side on the backswing before swinging your arms back down in front of your body, through impact and into a tall finish. For golfers of all levels, tempo is the key to playing these shots well.

**1** The address position for hitting a fairway wood is very similar to that adopted when hitting the driver. The only exception is that the ball is obviously not placed on a tee peg for a shot played from the fairway and instead is played a fraction further back in the stance, an inch or so inside the left heel. Keep your weight evenly balanced between both feet.

**2** Many golfers run into trouble at the start of the swing when hitting a fairway wood shot. It is important to maintain full control from the outset, since the length of the club and the fast swing speed make it difficult to compensate for faults later in the swing.

A good swing thought to focus on is of sweeping the clubhead away low to the ground during the first few feet of the backswing – almost as though you are painting a line along the ground with the sole of the club. This ensures that your tempo remains smooth and that you create a wide and powerful swing arc as your weight begins to move across onto your right side. Focus on making a full backswing for good rhythm and power.

# Hitting your long, mid- and short irons more effectively

While your fairway woods and driver are designed to strike the ball ever so slightly on the upswing, your irons produce the best results with a descending blow. The aim is to squeeze the ball between the turf and the clubface at impact, thereby propelling the ball forwards.

A good way to experience the sensations required at impact is to rehearse this particular part of the swing. Take up your normal address position, then move your left knee towards the target, rotate your left hip behind you and push your hands just ahead of the ball. This will give you a good example of how much pressure you apply to the ball at the point of impact, although in reality, the force applied will be much greater.

Contrary to what you might think, you do not need to make a different swing for each club in the bag. The swing technique required for hitting a 3-iron, for example, is exactly the same as that used when hitting a pitching wedge. The only discernible difference between the two swings is that the posture at address will be slightly different, since you will stand a little more upright at address when hitting a 3-iron than when playing a pitching wedge because the clubs are different in length. Other than that, the only difference is that the swing momentum you create with the longer irons will enable you to swing the club into a position where the shaft is almost horizontal to the ground and aiming square to the target at the top of your backswing, while your shorter irons will come up just short of horizontal and aim a little to the left of the target. This is perfectly normal.

| **3-iron** | **6-iron** | **pitching wedge** |

**1** When hitting one of your long irons, the length of the club and the resultant momentum of the swing will allow you to reach a position where the clubshaft is almost horizontal to the ground and aiming directly square to, or a touch left of, the intended target line.

**2** Many observers would mistakenly say that this club is 'laid-off' (aiming left of the target line), but the clubshaft is actually in the perfect position for a mid-iron – just short of horizontal and aiming slightly left of the target line. If the player chose to continue her swing, the shaft would aim square to the target.

**3** The relatively short length of this clubshaft makes it virtually impossible to swing the club into a position where it is horizontal to the ground and aiming square to the intended target without losing control over the shot. As a rule, a three-quarter length swing for a pitching wedge is just about perfect.

# Shaping your shots

Once your game has developed to the stage where you can strike the ball consistently well, your next step is to learn how to shape your shots. You may think that the top professionals hit every ball as straight as an arrow, but more often than not, they will curve the ball in the air; this is known as fading or drawing the ball. A fade is where the ball starts off slightly left of target and curves back to the right, while the draw starts out right before curving back to the left in the air.

Some players have a swing that naturally produces either shape. Scotland's Mhairi McKay, for example, naturally draws the ball, which means that her swing creates a right-to-left flight. Janice Moodie, on the other hand, prefers to fade the ball with a slight left-to-right flight.

You will probably find that you favour one shape of shot or the other, but it will benefit your game if you can master the fade and the draw. Shaping your shots enables you to work the ball into a tricky pin position on the green, for example, or cut off a chunk of a dog-leg hole from the tee.

## The fade

When asked why he hit a fade with every shot, Lee Trevino once said: 'You can talk to a fade, but a draw won't listen'. By that he meant that a fade is more controllable than a draw. It produces a shot with more backspin so the ball lands softly and is less likely to run into trouble. To produce the left-to-right flight, the clubface cuts across the ball from out-to-in.

**1** Aim the clubface at your intended target – normally the pin – and then position your body so that your feet, hips and shoulders all aim a few degrees to the left. The further left you aim, the more the ball will curve in the air.

**2** Once you have set up slightly open (aiming left) to the target line, commit to swinging the club along the line of your feet and shoulders.

**3** Hold the clubface square to the target through impact as you swing through. Do not release your right forearm too quickly. Think of a drop shot in tennis – where you cut underneath the ball so that it stops stone dead on landing.

### Fade Pointers

- Aim clubface where you want the ball to finish – usually near the hole on the green
- Aim your feet, hips and shoulders to the left of the intended target
- Commit to swinging the club along the line of your feet and body during the swing
- Hold the clubface square to your intended target as you swing through impact

**4** The ball will start off to the left of the target, following an extension of the path of your swing before curving back to the right in the air to finish up where the clubface was aiming at address.

## QUICK TIP

### Make left-handed swing to feel the fade

A good way to experience how the position at impact should feel when hitting a fade shot, is to make some practice swings holding the club with just your left hand. As you swing the club through impact, focus on keeping the back of your left hand or your watch face pointing towards the target. Do not allow your left forearm to turn over so that the watch face or the back of your hand faces the ground. Holding the clubface open through impact combined with swinging across the target line to the left will ensure that the clubface cuts across the ball to impart the left-to-right spin.

## The draw

Although it is a natural shape of shot for many golfers, other top players will intentionally draw the ball when they are looking for extra distance, since the topspin on the shot causes the ball to roll more than usual on landing. Continuing with the tennis analogy from the previous page, if the fade is the drop shot, the draw is the top-spin forehand winner. The key to the shot is for your right forearm to release more aggressively to help close the clubface through impact and impart the right-to-left spin on the ball.

A draw is useful if you want to play an approach shot to a pin that is tucked away in the far left corner of a green or if you want to take full advantage of a dog-leg hole that curves round to the left off the tee. Even players whose natural shot is the fade should look to master the draw, as the ability to move the ball either way improves your versatility and increases your options when considering which shot to play.

The only downside of the draw is that it is a shot that can easily get out of control. There is a thin dividing line between a controlled draw and an uncontrollable hook shot, so you must be careful not to exaggerate the address position and the swing, which is illustrated below. Used effectively, a draw can be a powerful addition to your golfing armoury, but you should always remember that a draw will generally run further on landing than a fade and is, therefore, more likely to end up in trouble.

**1** Aim the clubface at your intended target, but unlike the fade where you aim your body to the left, this time close your stance slightly so that your feet, hips and shoulders all aim right of where you want the ball to finish.

**2** Swing the club along the line of your body just as though you were going to hit a shot well to the right of your intended target. Your closed stance will make it easier for you to make a complete backswing.

**3** Do not be afraid to release your right forearm through impact in exactly the same way that you would hit a forehand down the line in tennis. Rotate your right forearm over the left through the hitting area to close the clubface in relation to the line of the swing.

### Draw Pointers

- Aim the clubface at your intended target
- Aim your feet, hips and shoulders right of line
- Commit to swinging along the line of your body in the backswing and downswing
- Release the clubface by rotating your right forearm

**4** Allow your right side to fire through as you release the clubface at impact. You must commit to the shot, otherwise the ball will fly straight right and will not curve back to the left in the air as you want it to.

## QUICK TIP

### Hit a forehand top-spin winner

While the fade can be compared to the drop shot in tennis, the draw is the top-spin forehand winner down the line. To experience the swing feelings associated with the draw through impact, hold the club with your right hand and make some practice swings focusing on the feeling of hitting a forehand top-spin shot down the line. You will need to fire your right shoulder through towards the target and rotate your right forearm freely through impact as you release the club.

# Sloping lies

The major problem that slopes present is that they move the ball from its normal position in the stance – either further forward or back, or higher or lower – leaving most golfers unsure of what to do next. Given the option of adjusting their address position or improvising their swing to reach the ball, most players wrongly take the latter option.

The key to playing from any kind of slope – uphill, downhill or sidehill – is to set up in such a way that you can still use your normal swing to play the shot. It is better to adjust your address position than to manufacture a swing that you have never tried before. When the ball is above your feet, for example, you should stand a little more upright and choke down on the grip to compensate for the fact that the ball is nearer your body. When the ball is below your feet the opposite approach should be taken.

On uphill and downhill lies, the first thing to do is amend your set-up so that your shoulders are as close as possible to level with the slope in question. By doing this, you effectively recreate a flat lie, which enables you to use your normal swing to play the shot.

Your final consideration when playing from any kind of slope is that you should swing as smoothly as possible. Any time you are confronted with a shot that is slightly out of the norm, the temptation is to swing too quickly to get it over and done with and the end result is usually less than impressive, leading to an even greater lack of confidence the next time. A smooth tempo will often compensate for technical flaws in your swing, so even if you are unsure about how to amend your address position, if you can remain calm enough to swing smoothly you will have a good chance of playing the shot.

## Ball above feet

When the ball is above the level of your feet, you should stand more upright at address and choke down on the grip of the club. Your more upright spine angle will produce a flatter and more rounded swing path, which will cause the ball to curve from right to left in the air. Allow for this by aiming right of your intended target.

## Ball below feet

When the ball is below your feet, it is further away from you. Allow for this by tilting forwards more with your body, increasing your knee flex and gripping the club towards the end of the handle. The tendency is to swing the club on a steep plane, which produces a shot that flies from left to right. Allow for this by aiming left of your intended target.

## Uphill lie

On an uphill lie, you have a ready-made launch pad to help get the ball airborne, so remember to allow for the higher ball flight by taking a less-lofted club to achieve a similar distance as you would from a flat lie. To bring your shoulders in line with the slope, place a little extra weight on your right leg at address and keep your right shoulder low. This will allow you to swing along and up the slope through impact, rather than straight into it.

## Downhill lie

When the ball is on a downslope, the gradient removes loft from the clubface, thereby causing the ball to follow a lower trajectory. Allow for this by selecting a slightly more lofted club to play the shot. In this case, when you bring your shoulders in line with the slope you automatically set a little extra weight on your left side. Feel as though your left shoulder is lower than normal at address, even to the point where it feels lower than the right. From this address position, the steeper takeaway will enable you to comfortably clear the slope on your backswing.

### 'Ball Above Feet' Pointers
- Stand taller at address
- Choke down on grip
- Aim right of your intended target as the more rounded swing plane will cause the ball to curve to the left in the air
- Take one club less, since the right-to-left spin will cause the ball to travel further than normal

### 'Ball Below Feet' Pointers
- Tilt forwards more with upper body
- Increase the flex in your knees
- Aim left of your intended target, as the more upright swing plane will cause the ball to curve from left-to-right in the air
- Select one club higher than normal to compensate for slice spin on the ball

### 'Uphill Lie' Pointers
- Take one extra club to allow for the extra loft at address
- Place more weight on right side at address to bring shoulders more in line with the slope
- Play the ball further forward in stance
- Set right shoulder well below the left

### 'Downhill Lie' Pointers
- Take a more lofted club to allow for lower trajectory
- Place more weight on left side at address to bring shoulders in line with the slope
- Play ball further back in stance to improve chances of making crisp contact
- Set left shoulder well below the right

# Faults and fixes

Almost every problem that occurs when playing from a sloping lie stems from either a lack of understanding of how the slope in question will affect the flight, shape and trajectory of the ball, or simply by addressing the ball normally and attempting to manufacture a swing to counteract the effects of the slope. If, for example, you are playing a shot where the ball is below the level of your feet and you stand to the ball normally, it stands to reason that you will somehow have to lower yourself down to reach the ball at impact. Rather than trying to dip into the ball during your downswing, it will obviously be far easier for you to lower yourself at address so that you can then make a normal swing and make contact with the ball solidly at impact.

Likewise, if you are playing a shot from a slope where the ball is above your feet and nearer to you than normal, instead of adopting your standard address position and then somehow trying to make room to swing the club through impact, it is far easier to choke down on the grip at address and stand a little taller so that you will be able to strike the ball cleanly without changing your swing.

## FAULT

### • Mishit shots from a sloping lie

The most common mistake when playing from a sloping lie is neglecting to adjust the address position, and the result is that it becomes almost impossible to make your normal swing without the slope getting in the way.

The key to playing from uphill and downhill lies is setting the shoulders as square as possible to the slope in question so that the golfer can swing normally with the contours rather than fighting against them.

In this photograph, the golfer has addressed the ball normally with her shoulders fairly level even though she is playing from a severe downslope. From this position, it is almost impossible for her to make her backswing without swinging the club straight back into the slope.

## *FIX*

### • *Adjust the set-up not the swing*

Although it may initially feel very strange and awkward, it is vital that every adjustment that you make when playing from a sloping lie is carried out at the set-up stage. From a downslope like this, the first thing to do is adjust your shoulders so that they are positioned as level as possible to the slope at address. In the case illustrated in the photographs below, most of the player's weight is positioned on her front foot, which will inevitably lead to a fairly steep backswing.

Another key to playing from slopes is to allow your clubhead to trace the contours of the ground, so that you swing with the slope rather than fight against it. From a downhill lie, it is very important to keep the clubhead as low to the ground as possible in the downswing, even to the extent that you feel as though the clubhead chases the ball down the slope. Otherwise it is all too easy to catch the ball thin.

Your final consideration is that the downslope effectively delofts the clubface at impact, so you will need to take a slightly more lofted club than normal to help get the ball in the air.

# *Power out of the rough*

The first thing you should consider when playing a shot out of thick and heavy rough, is that you should never underestimate the resistance that the grass will put up against your swing. Even the light, fluffy fringe grass – or semi rough – that you often find lurking inconspicuously just off the edge of the fairway is enough to get between the ball and the clubface, taking a considerable number of yards off your shot.

Many women golfers struggle to generate power from the tee or fairway when the ball is lying cleanly, so when the ball is nestled down a couple of inches in thick grass, it is hardly surprising that these same golfers find it extremely difficult to get the ball out and travelling toward the target with any degree of authority.

### Never underestimate the resistance of the grass

The first thing you must accept when hitting out of the rough is that there is no substitute for strength. There are certain techniques that you can use to make the shot easier, but ultimately power plays a key role in removing your ball from the rough. You have to swing hard. Unfortunately, there is no other option available.

Secondly, you should try to create a steeper attack into the ball in the downswing so that you avoid swinging the clubhead through lots and lots of thick and heavy grass in front of the ball that will inevitably slow your swing speed down considerably. With this in mind, you will find it helpful to set up with a little extra weight on your left side; this will make it easier for you to hit down on the ball through impact. Most top players will also open the clubface at address because they know that the grass is likely to wrap itself around the clubhead through impact, closing the face and producing a low, squirty shot that travels sharply to the left, usually into even deeper trouble.

Once you have made these amendments to your address position, pick the club up fairly steeply in your backswing and then concentrate on hitting purposefully down and through. One hundred per cent commitment is essential, since anything less than a full swing will make it difficult for you to achieve any great distance.

My last piece of advice concerning this type of shot concerns your course management and your ability to weigh up the risks involved when playing out of the rough and to think realistically. Many amateur golfers underestimate how much the thick rough will affect their shot, and they still believe that they can hit the ball almost as far as they can from the fairway. Unfortunately, that is not the case – usually even for the likes of Se Ri Pak or Karrie Webb. Check your ego before attempting to blast the ball out of heavy grass. Unless your ball is lying perfectly and sitting up nicely in thick rough, do not even think about playing anything other than one of your wedges or a mid-iron at most. It is just not worth the risk. Nine times out of ten the sensible strategy is to get the ball safely back on to the fairway.

**1** To avoid swinging the clubhead through lots of thick grass in front of the ball, play the ball back in your stance, pick the club up steeply in your backswing and hit down sharply.

## Rough Pointers

- Set extra weight on front foot at address to create a steeper attack into the ball
- Grass will twist clubface into a closed position at impact so compensate by opening face at address
- Hold on tighter with left hand to keep clubface square through impact
- Do not get too adventurous, think safety first

## Allow for a 'flyer' out of the semi rough or fringe grass

While it can often be difficult to move the ball even a few yards out of thick rough, at the other end of the scale, very light rough or fringe grass just off the edge of the fairway can actually help you hit the ball further. When thin blades of grass become trapped between the clubface and the ball at impact they reduce the amount of friction created between the grooves and the cover of the golf ball and, in turn, the amount of backspin imparted. As a result, the ball leaves the clubface very quickly and flies further through the air. This is known as a 'flyer'. Unfortunately, it is very difficult to predict a flyer, but there are times when you may need to guard against one; for example when there is a water hazard just beyond the green.

## QUICK TIP

### Hold on tight with the left hand

One of the problems with playing out of thick rough is that the grass wraps itself around the clubface at impact. One way to guard against this is to grip a little tighter with your left hand as you play the shot. Increasing your grip pressure will prevent the grass from twisting the clubface into a closed position at impact, which causes the ball to shoot off to the left. With a firmer grip you can hold the clubface in a much squarer position.

**2** Depending on the lie, you will probably have to hold on to the club tightly through impact to stop the thick grass twisting the face into a closed position. Commit to the shot and never decelerate the clubhead through impact.

**3** Make it your goal to swing through into a decent length follow-through. You may struggle to release the club and the rough will inevitably restrict your swing, but you should always accelerate the clubhead purposefully through impact.

# *The fairway bunker shot*

Hitting a full shot from a fairway bunker can be a terrifying prospect for many amateur golfers. Even accomplished low handicappers and professionals will view the shot with a great deal of respect because the margin for error is tiny. If you catch the ground first when playing a shot from a decent lie in the fairway, you will probably still be able to hit the ball a fair distance. If you do the same thing in a bunker, however, the heavy resistance of the sand can stop a fast-moving clubhead stone-dead in its tracks. The end result is low swing speed and

very little distance. You will be lucky to remove the ball from the bunker, let alone get it to the green.

Maintaining your height, spine angle and knee flex are the keys to consistent ball striking and that philosophy is just as applicable to playing from a fairway bunker, since any loss of height will cause the clubhead to dig into the sand before the ball. Keeping your swing as smooth and controlled as possible while avoiding sudden changes in swing speed and lunges at the ball, will ensure successful fairway bunker play.

**1** Your priority is to ensure that the clubhead does not make contact with the sand before the ball. Set up as though you are going to play a shot from the fairway. Avoid shuffling your feet into the sand as that will lower your body and increase your chances of catching the shot heavy. Straighten your legs slightly to raise the clubhead off the ground.

**2** As you make your swing it is important to maintain your height. Focus on keeping the flex in your knees and your spine angle consistent all the way through from start to finish. If your body bobs up and down, the shot will become very difficult.

## *Fairway Bunker Pointers*

- Avoid hitting the sand
- Set up as though playing a normal shot from the fairway
- Straighten legs slightly to raise clubhead at address
- Maintain height and knee flex throughout swing
- Keep tempo even-paced

**3** With little margin for error at impact, it is a good idea to keep your rhythm and tempo as smooth and even-paced as possible. If you can avoid sudden lunges or dramatic changes in your swing speed, you will stand a much better chance of staying in control of the shot and clipping the ball neatly off the top of the sand.

### QUICK TIP

## Think 'thin' to win

From a fairway bunker, you are ideally looking to clip the ball cleanly off the top of the sand. However, this is one time when catching the ball slightly thin is not too disastrous. If the leading edge of the clubface strikes the ball too near its centre, the outcome is normally a low, piercing shot with very little control. If you are close to the green this is obviously not desirable, but from a fairway bunker a long way out, it is not too much of a problem. In fact, it may even help generate a little extra distance for you. If you are not confident of striking the ball cleanly, err on the side of caution, play for a thin and let a poor strike help you out.

# *The Short Game*

**E**xactly where the long game ends and the short game begins is a matter of some debate. In my opinion, the cut-off point is the distance where a player has to make a less than full swing to reach the green. For most women, this means that the short game takes over at around 60yds out. Coincidentally, statistics show that over two-thirds of the shots in an average round of golf are played from within this range.

Because of the wide variety of different courses, together with variables such as the pin position, the size, shape and contours of the putting surface and the lie of the ball, there are an infinite number of shots you can face around the greens. Unfortunately, you only have half-a-dozen or so suitable clubs at your disposal, so vision and imagination play a key role in an accomplished short game. Without the ability to picture a shot in your mind, you will stand little chance of executing it successfully.

# Pitching: your number one short game ally

Pitching is the term used to describe a shot played into the green using slightly less than a full swing. Sounds easy, but many women golfers regard a 50yd pitch from the fairway with the same trepidation as a bunker shot.

On the face of it, the pitch shot seems the easier option, but many golfers struggle with their pitching because they feel uncomfortable shortening their swing. Players who are unsure how to play the shot, either speed up their rhythm to compensate for their shorter backswing, or they swing too lazily and leave the ball short of their intended target. One thing to remember is that there is no magical secret; the pitch shot is simply an abbreviation of the full swing.

**1** Because you are looking for accuracy rather than power, bring your feet closer together, stand a little nearer the ball and choke down on the club. Some coaches recommend that you open your stance a little (aim left with your feet and hips) to give yourself room to swing the club through impact, but this is not strictly necessary. For the regular pitch shot, the ball should be played in the centre of the stance with the weight distributed evenly between the feet.

**2** As for the swing itself, your priority is to maintain the angles you create with your knees and lower back all the way back and through. Most pitch shots are fluffed when the golfer tries to scoop the ball into the air and inadvertently straightens her legs and/or her upper body. When this happens it is very easy to catch the ball thin or heavy. If you can maintain your height throughout the swing, however, you stand a good chance of making crisp contact with the ball.

**3** Good tempo is an attribute that many women golfers possess, but if you are an anxious pitcher it is still easy to fall into the trap of rushing the shot. You do not want to mollycoddle the ball towards the hole, either. Pitch shots must be played authoritatively. Watch the world's top players and you will see that they commit totally to the shot, safe in the knowledge that the narrow stance, shorter backswing and lofted club will prevent them from hitting the ball too far.

# How to judge distance

Once you have mastered the basic pitching action, your next step is to enhance your distance control. Great pitching technique without control is worthless. Judging distance is probably the most difficult aspect of the short game for most amateurs. While Tour professionals are constantly working on their touch and feel through daily play and practice, the chances are that you will not have that luxury and will need a few short cuts.

### Use hips, chest and shoulders as reference points.

Many of the top professionals will rely on their feel to help them judge the distance of these short-range shots, but for most amateurs it will help to know how far you can carry the ball using different length backswings. Using your hips, chest and shoulders as reference points will help you develop more control.

### Do not limit yourself to your wedges.

Do not think that just because you are hitting a pitch shot you must automatically use your pitching wedge. On the contrary, you can play these shots with anything from an 8-iron to a lob wedge, depending on how far you need to hit the ball and how quickly you need it to stop when it reaches the green. Extra pitching clubs at your disposal means more options.

### Vary your clubhead release.

Another way to control the distance you hit your pitch shot, is to vary the release of the clubhead through the ball. Many top players consciously hold the clubface open through impact to impart more backspin and control on the ball so that it stops quickly. However, you can also rotate your forearms more aggressively through the hitting area to make the ball roll further on landing.

## USE HIPS, CHEST AND SHOULDERS TO JUDGE DISTANCE

### Three swing checkpoints and three different clubs give nine distances

A simple way to improve your distance control is to find out how far you can pitch the ball when you swing your hands back to hip height, chest height and shoulder height. This will give you three base yardages from which you should be able to make an educated guess at distances for most pitch shots. It is also a good idea to know how far you can hit the ball with, say, your 9-iron, pitching wedge and sand wedge. Combine these three basic yardages with the three different clubs and all of a sudden you have nine different distances that you can hit the ball. Make a note of your yardages and review them regularly.

# *Chipping*

You may be surprised to learn that even the world's best players only manage to find 13 or 14 greens in regulation during an average round. That means that, on a good day, the likes of Annika Sorenstam, Karrie Webb and Dottie Pepper will need to chip and putt, or pitch and putt, for a par at least four or five times. So just imagine how many times you will find yourself in a similar situation. In all probability you will need to rely on your short game at least 12 or 13 times per round.

That may sound depressing, but think of it as an opportunity for you to shave shots off your handicap. Just imagine the difference it would make to your score if you could get up and down in two shots just 50 per cent of the time, or if you never took more than three shots to get the ball into the hole from within 70yds out.

## *Your short game tools*

To give yourself the best possible chance of developing a razor sharp short game, you will need the right tools. Most of the world's top women golfers nowadays carry three or four different wedges in their bag to cope with the multitude of situations that can occur around the greens. In addition to the standard pitching wedge and sand wedge, there are also middle wedges and lob wedges featuring varying amounts of extra loft. These clubs give you extra options when faced with an awkward situation. A 60-degree lob wedge, for example, is perfect for playing shots where you need to get the ball up in the air quickly and land it softly on the green. Before the introduction of the lob wedge, the only way to play that particular shot was to lay the face of a sand wedge wide open and make a long, lazy swing. Most amateur golfers, quite understandably, found this shot rather difficult.

However, adding one or two extra wedges to your set means that a couple of other clubs will have to make way. Many women struggle with their longer irons and, because of that, the 3-iron and 4-iron are the least used clubs, making just a few appearances per round. Consider sacrificing one or two long irons in favour of the more versatile 'scoring' wedges.

## *What comes first: touch or technique?*

Many golfers claim that a good 'touch' is the key to a good short game. Although there is much truth in that statement, it does not tell the whole story. Good feel originates from consistency, which stems from a solid technique. Only when you are confident that the ball will leave the clubface in the same way each time, is it possible to develop your feel for distance. If you struggle to make clean contact with the ball, getting it close to the hole from around the green comes down to luck.

A chip shot is generally played from just a few yards off the green. It requires a short swing back and through, and it is intended to loft the ball over the longer grass and onto the putting surface, where it runs along the green to the hole.

*Right:* Only once you have developed a consistent and repetitive chipping action can you start to develop your touch and feel around the greens.

**1** Choking down on the grip by a few inches will give you more control over the shot and reduce the distance you can hit the ball.

**2** Set up with your weight favouring your left side and with your hands ahead of the ball, which should be played towards the back foot.

**3** You stand closer to the ball for a chip shot than for a full swing. Open your stance a little so that you have room to swing the club through impact.

## The chip and run

Before you attempt to play any fancy and adventurous chip shots around the green, you first need a stock shot that will serve you in a variety of situations. Only once you have mastered the basic chipping action, can you start to experiment with your set-up and swing in order to play the more specialist recoveries that you see demonstrated by the top professionals on Tour.

The chip and run (also known as the bump and run) is the simplest and the most consistent chip shot. It is usually played when there are no obstacles blocking your path to the green. A no-frills shot, the general idea is to loft the ball over the fringe grass and onto the putting surface so that it rolls the rest of the way to the hole along the ground. Although it is a simple shot to play, many amateurs struggle to master it because they fail to adhere to a few basic ground rules in the address position.

## Setting up for a chip and run

The set-up is the secret to good chipping. There is no need for a wide stance because you are not trying to hit the ball a long way, so place your feet fairly close together and shuffle a little closer to the ball. Depending on the length of the shot facing you, you may also need to grip the club further down the shaft than normal, as this will give you a greater sense of control over the shot as well as reduce the distance that you can hit the ball. Play the ball towards the centre of your stance, keep your weight evenly distributed between both feet, and make sure that your hands are just in front of the ball. If anything, your weight should fractionally favour your left side, as this will help you hit down on the ball through impact. All of these amendments to your normal address position will help you produce a low-running shot. Your hands simply lead the clubface through impact to nip the ball off the turf with a little check spin for ultimate control.

# The chipping technique

Once you have set up correctly, the chip shot is played mainly with the arms and shoulders. It is not a good idea to introduce too much wrist action, as this creates unnecessary height on the shot and can lead to inconsistency with your ball striking. It is perfectly acceptable for your wrists to yield a little in response to the weight and momentum of the clubhead, but make sure that this hand action does not develop into the disastrous 'scooping' motion that ruins so many scores for amateur golfers. With your weight favouring your front foot, swing the club away with your arms and shoulders.

Your weight should remain on your front foot all the way through the swing, as any kind of weight transference during what is a fairly short and brisk motion will inevitably make it difficult to strike the ball crisply. Keep the movement as compact as possible, and as you swing your arms back down, make sure that your hands remain passive and ahead of the ball through impact for a crisp strike. A good swing thought to focus on is of returning to your original address position at impact, as this will ensure that your hands lead the clubface through the ball.

**1** Set up with your weight favouring your front foot and the ball back in a fairly narrow stance to maximize your chances of striking the ball crisply and to produce a low-running shot.

**2** Your weight stays on your front foot as you swing the club away with your arms and shoulders. Do not allow your wrists to hinge too much on the backswing as this will cause problems later.

## Chipping Pointers

- Stance is fairly narrow with weight favouring front foot
- Ball should be played slightly further back than normal
- Keep the swing short and compact where possible
- Keep weight on front foot throughout the shot
- Hands should lead the clubface through impact

**3** Swing your arms back to their original starting position, focusing on keeping your hands ahead of the ball at impact to guarantee a crisp, clean strike. The key to good chipping is accelerating the clubhead through impact with your hands ahead of the ball.

## CLUB SELECTION

Once you have mastered the basic chipping action, your next step is selecting the right club. There are no hard and fast rules here. Many top players, for example, have a favourite club with which they will confidently play most of their shots around the green. Other golfers believe that being able to choose from several different clubs offers them more flexibility.

Your ultimate goal should be to become confident hitting chip shots with anything from a 4-iron to a lob wedge. The straighter-faced clubs will not carry the ball as far through the air, but will stay closer to the ground and run considerably further upon landing. The more lofted clubs produce higher-flying and softer-landing shots. Experiment around the greens with a variety of different clubs and note the difference in flight, trajectory and roll. The results should be something like this:

| Club | Carry | Roll |
| --- | --- | --- |
| 4-iron | 10 per cent | 90 per cent |
| 6-iron | 30 per cent | 70 per cent |
| 8-iron | 50 per cent | 50 per cent |
| pitching wedge | 70 per cent | 30 per cent |
| lob wedge | 90 per cent | 10 per cent |

# *Planning your chip shots*

The ability to visualize a shot plays a vital role in successful chipping. Most top players will attempt, where possible, to land the ball first bounce onto the putting surface when playing a chip shot. The reason for this is that it is difficult to predict exactly how the ball will react if it lands in long fringe grass or rough. It could skip onto the green perfectly, or it could just as easily snag and barely make it onto the putting surface. It is a variable that places doubt in your mind as you stand over the ball.

Once you know what ratio of carry and roll you can expect with each club, planning your shots becomes easier. All you need do is decide which club will loft the ball onto the green and still produce enough roll to get it to the hole. If your ball is just a couple of feet off the green, a straighter-faced chipping club will pop it over the fringe and enable it to roll the rest of the way. However, if you are further away, you will need a more lofted club; exactly which one depends on how far you are from the green and, from there, the distance to the hole.

**1** The world's top golfers actively look to hole their chip shots and you should be just as positive. Pay as much attention to a chip as you would to a putt. To get these shots close you need to read the break and borrow on the greens.

**2** When planning your chip shot, it's a good idea to walk to a point roughly halfway between the ball and the hole to get a better perspective of the distance. You will also be able to see how the ball will break nearer to the flag.

**3** Once you have assessed the break and the line of the shot, make several practice swings – ideally while looking at the hole – to get a feel for the length of backswing you will need to get the ball to the hole.

## Chipping Pointers
- Read chips like putts
- Look to hole your chip shots
- Always visualize the shot before playing it
- Make plenty of practice strokes while looking at the target to enhance your sense of distance
- Commit to the shot

**4** Once you have finished your pre-shot preparation, trust your initial instincts and commit to playing the shot as you planned and visualized it. Never quit on the ball through impact.

## PRACTICE TIP

### Experiment with different clubs

Never be afraid to experiment with your short game. Trying out different shots on the practice ground will help you find out what is possible and, just as importantly, what is not. Knowing how the ball will react with different clubs and from different lies is invaluable. To familiarize yourself with the characteristics of all your chipping irons, spend some time hitting shots with each club and noting how high the ball flies and how far it rolls when it hits the green. You will soon find that a chip shot played with a lofted club such as a sand wedge will fly high and land quickly, while a shot played with a 5-iron will leave the clubface at a much lower angle and run considerably further when it hits the green. Once you have absorbed this basic knowledge you will be able to experiment with different clubface and ball positions to produce a whole range of shots around the green. Knowledge like this forms the foundation of your short game.

# Faults and fixes

### • Taking the wrong option around the green

One of the classic amateur errors when chipping from around the green is taking on a more complicated shot than is necessary. From just off the fringe like this, there is no need whatsoever for such a long backswing. With no obstacles blocking her route to the hole, a fairly short and compact swing with very little wrist action is the more sensible option.

Hitting the higher shot will not necessarily end in disaster, but there is greater margin for error when the wrists are involved in the swing, because it is more difficult to control the length of the shot.

### • Never make a long swing when a short swing will do

If you watch the world's top golfers around the greens, you will notice that they always take the simple option if it is available. Hitting a higher shot requires a longer backswing and more wrist action; two variables that add extra risk to the shot. In this situation, the best option is to play a simple bump and run with a 5-iron. By employing a fairly short and compact backswing, you can nudge the ball over the fringe onto the green and watch the ball run the rest of the way to the hole along the ground. All things considered, it is a safer option.

## FAULT

### • *Wristy chips are risky chips*

Many women golfers commit the cardinal chipping sin of trying to scoop the ball up into the air when playing a chip shot rather than letting the loft on the clubface do the work. When you start trying to add extra loft with your hands, you bring all kinds of problems into play. For a start, it suddenly becomes easy for the leading edge of the clubface to catch the middle of the ball and send it racing through the green at 100mph. It is also easy to stub the club into the ground before striking the ball. In short, all kinds of disaster shots are possible once you start 'flicking' with your hands.

## FIX

### • *Place a club on the ground behind ball*

A good way to prevent getting too wristy through impact is to place a club on the ground about 15cm (6in) behind the ball. The club will encourage you to hit down on the ball instead of flicking at it with your hands; an action that would cause you to strike the shaft of the club on the ground before the ball. It will be easier to strike the ball cleanly if you set a little extra weight onto your left side at address, as this will create a steeper angle of attack in the downswing and enable you to avoid the club on the ground.

# The downhill chip shot

This is a shot that terrifies many amateur golfers, but which is actually far easier than it looks, providing you remember two key facts and approach the ball with a degree of confidence. Firstly, keep in mind that the ball will shoot off low and fast from this type of lie, so you will need to use a lofted club such as a pitching wedge or, depending on how hard the ground is, a sand wedge or a lob wedge. Secondly, you must alter your normal set-up to avoid swinging the clubhead straight back into the slope.

As with a full shot from a sloping lie, the key to chipping successfully from a downslope is setting your shoulders square to the ground so that you can swing with the slope rather than against it. With your weight set on your front foot, maintain your height during the backswing and then concentrate on keeping the clubface low to the ground in the downswing. It will help if the lie is soft and fluffy, as this enables you to slide the clubhead underneath the ball without fear of it bouncing off the ground into the back of the ball.

**1** Set your shoulders as square as possible to the ground. In this case, you will have to set extra weight on your front foot to bring your shoulders in line with the ground. Many top golfers also increase the flex in their left leg to give them more stability. You can also choke down on the grip for more control.

**2** With your weight set firmly on your left side, the secret to playing this shot well is to allow your swing to follow the contours of the slope. The fact that the majority of your weight will be on your left side means that your backswing will be a little steeper than normal. Maintain your height and your balance.

**3** Your priority is to ensure that the clubhead traces the slope in the downswing, even to the point where you feel that it chases down the slope after the ball has left the clubface. Focus on holding the flex in your left knee to ensure that you maintain your height and avoid catching the ball thin.

## Downhill Chip Pointers

- Set shoulders level with slope with weight on front foot
- Create a steep backswing
- Increase flex in knees to lower your body
- Keep clubhead low to the ground in downswing
- Open the clubface for a softer landing and more control

**4** Resist all temptation to scoop the ball into the air with your hands through impact. Hold all the angles that you introduced at address throughout the swing, and focus on keeping the clubhead low to the ground in the downswing all the way through to end in a full finish.

## QUICK TIP

### Open the clubface for an extra-soft landing

A downslope effectively removes loft from the clubface, so the ball will always fly at a lower angle than normal. This can make the shot very difficult to control, particularly if you need to stop the ball quickly once it lands on the green. A good way to soften the shot is to open the face of your wedge to add extra loft to the clubface. If you combine the open clubface with a little extra wrist action and soft hands on the backswing, you should find that you can gently pop the ball up in the air.

# The lob shot

As a general rule, it is advisable to keep the ball low to the ground when chipping from around the green, but there are times when bunkers and bushes, ditches and streams conspire to give you only a small area of the green to land the ball on. In such situations, where you need to get the ball up in the air quickly and land it softly, the lob shot is your only option.

The lob shot is, however, a higher risk shot than the basic bump and run and should only be played when there is no safer alternative. It is not a shot that works well off tight, dry or bare lies and you must commit 100 per cent to the swing. There are no half measures. To make matters worse for many amateur golfers, the technique required to execute the shot is very similar to that used when playing out of a bunker. However, once you are confident playing the shot, you will find yourself looking for excuses to play it time and time again because it is a fun shot to play and highly impressive, too.

**1** Open the face of your sand or lob wedge then grip the club so that it remains open during the swing. Open your stance so that your feet, hips and shoulders all aim left of the target. Play the ball well forward between your feet, with the clubface aiming at, or slightly right of, the target.

**2** Swing back along the line of your feet into a full backswing. You have to make a swing of this length to generate forward momentum on the shot.

**3** As you swing back down to the ball, hold the clubface open through impact to maximize the loft. Feel as though your right forearm stays below the left through the ball, and keep the grooves on the clubface aiming at the sky well into your follow-through. Accelerate the clubhead authoritatively through the grass.

### Lob Shot Pointers

- Only play the lob shot when there is no safer alternative
- Only play the lob shot out of fluffy or soft grass
- Open the clubface at address before you grip the club
- Commit to a long backswing and full follow-through

**4** A full follow-through is a sign of a well-played lob shot. Because of your open stance and the amount of loft on the clubface, you will need to swing through to a full finish to generate enough forward momentum on the shot.

### QUICK TIP

### Keep grooves facing the sky in follow-through

Maintaining maximum loft on the clubface is probably the most important key to playing the lob shot. If the clubface closes through impact or even remains square, you will not be able to generate sufficient height on the ball. One good swing thought to help you keep the clubface open through impact, is to focus on keeping the grooves on the clubface aiming at the sky all the way through the hitting area and into your follow-through. This ensures that the clubface stays open for as long as possible, adding height to the shot.

# Bunker Play

**T**here are two reasons why professionals do not regard bunkers with the same fear and trepidation as amateurs. Firstly, pros spend many hours practising their bunker play so that they are confident of hitting controlled splash shots. Secondly, they know that in the sand wedge they have a club that is specially designed to help them. Such is their confidence, most professionals would prefer to play from the sand than from thick greenside rough, where it is often difficult to judge how the ball will react off the clubface.

Bunker shots are unique in golf, in that the objective is not to hit the ball, but instead to remove a thin slither of sand that starts a couple of inches in front of the ball and finishes a couple of inches behind it. If the player removes that shallow divot of sand from the bunker, the ball will fly out with it. In this chapter, you will learn how to use your sand wedge to play controlled bunker shots with confidence.

# The sand wedge

Most modern sets of golf clubs come with a sand wedge, but if you are still playing with an old set or have compiled your own, you should purchase a sand wedge as soon as you can.

The sand wedge is an extremely important club, so take some time to acquaint yourself with its design. If you look at the sole of the club, you will notice that, unlike your other irons, the wide and heavy flange hangs lower than the leading edge; this is known as the 'bounce' angle. It is this particular characteristic that allows the clubhead to bounce or skim through the sand without digging in deeply. The lower the flange hangs below the leading edge, the greater the bounce.

You may have heard top professionals say that they open the face of their sand wedge in a bunker. They do this to accentuate the bounce angle on the sole. If you twist the clubface, you will see how this works, as the flange hangs even lower. A skilled bunker player will vary the amount she opens the clubface to alter the distance she can hit the ball. It can also be varied to suit different lies and textures of sand.

# How to grip the club correctly

Your sand wedge is at its most effective when the clubface is in a slightly open position. Many amateurs make the mistake of taking their normal grip with the clubface in its usual square position, then attempt to open the clubface by turning both hands to the right. However, the end result is that the clubface closes through impact, causing the leading edge to dig too deeply into the sand as the hands release the club.

The correct way to grip your sand wedge is to firstly swivel the face into an open position. Now apply your left hand to the club, ensuring that the clubface remains open and does not revert back to its square alignment. You can now add your right hand to the grip, safe in the knowledge that when you make your swing, the clubface will remain open through impact with the ball.

It may take a little time to get used to seeing the face of your sand wedge laid open once you have taken your grip, but that initial anxiety will soon disappear once you realize how much it will help your game.

*Below:* **The wide sole on the sand wedge enables it to skim through the sand with less resistance than a normal iron, thereby making it easier to remove the ball from the sand.**

**1** The correct way to grip the club for bunker play is to first swivel the face open by a few degrees with your fingers, and then apply your left hand to the grip.

**2** Make sure that the clubface remains open as you complete your left-hand grip and also as you add your right hand to the club.

# *Feel your sand wedge bounce through the sand*

To get a feeling for how the clubface remains open through impact and bounces through the sand, open the clubface, then grip the club with just your right hand. Now make some practice swings in a bunker without a ball, focusing on hitting the sand with the wide part of the club's sole, not the leading edge. It should almost feel as though you are hitting the sand with the back of the clubface.

If you do this correctly, you should be able to swing down and through the sand without the clubface digging in at all and preventing you from making a full follow-through. Once you get used to the basic idea, you can experiment by opening the clubface further and swinging at different speeds to see how much sand the club removes from the bunker.

When you step into a bunker for real on the golf course, you should be full of confidence knowing that you can take full advantage of the design of the club.

**1** Without a golf ball to distract you, step into a bunker, open up the clubface and then grip the club with just your right hand. Now make some one-handed practice swings.

**2** Focus on splashing the clubface down confidently so that the wide part of the sole and not the leading edge makes contact with the sand. If the leading edge makes contact first the clubhead will dig in deeply.

**3** Ideally, you should be able to swing the club through to virtually a full follow-through. If you cannot make it through this far, then the leading edge of the clubface has dug too far into the sand.

# *Playing the splash shot*

## *The splash shot set-up*

Contrary to popular belief, there is nothing particularly complicated about how you should address the ball in a bunker. To compensate for the open clubface, you need to align your body slightly to the left of the target. How far left you aim depends on the distance you want to hit the ball. Open your stance slightly for a medium-length bunker shot, and increase the angle to play shots from shorter range. You will also need to shuffle your feet an inch or so down into the sand to give yourself a more stable footing, enabling you to stand on the harder base level of sand rather than the fluffier top layer.

Shuffling your feet down also lowers your whole body and, in turn, the base point of your swing. Consequently, the clubhead will enter the sand and slide right underneath the ball. Finally, you should remember to play the ball just forward of centre (in relation to the line of your swing, not the target line) in your stance.

**1** For a standard greenside bunker shot, the clubface should aim directly at, or slightly right of, the target while your feet, hips and shoulders all aim to the left. Shuffle your feet into the sand for a firm footing and to lower the base point of your swing.

**2** Play the ball forward in your stance so that you have plenty of room to splash the clubhead down into the sand behind the ball. Your stance should also be fairly wide to give yourself a solid base to your swing and to lower your body at address.

## The splash shot swing

Once you have made the necessary amendments to your address position, you have done most of the hard work. Playing the shot is no different to any other. However, you must remind yourself of the need to swing along the line of your feet and shoulders. All your hard work at address will count for nothing if instead of swinging along the line of your body, you decide to swing the club along the ball-target line. This will cause you problems because your swing will then be too flat in relation to your body alignment.

### Greenside Bunkers

- Open the face of your sand wedge before gripping the club
- Shuffle feet into the sand to lower the swing's base point
- Aim clubface at or slightly right of target line
- Aim feet, hips and shoulders left of the target line
- Accelerate the clubhead smoothly through impact

**1** Swing back along the line of your body, maintaining a smooth and even tempo, while keeping your weight evenly balanced between both feet. Allow your wrists to hinge naturally in response to the momentum and the weight of the clubhead. Good rhythm is vital for bunker shots. Always make a full backswing.

**2** Swing the club back down to the ball along the same path as the backswing and splash the clubface down into the sand. Allow the bounce and loft on the clubface to do all the work. Commitment is crucial as the heavy sand can stop a slow-moving swing dead. Accelerate the clubhead through impact.

**3** One sure sign of a good splash shot is a full follow-through. If you can make it through to a full finish like this, with your weight on your front foot, then it is highly likely that you have accelerated the clubhead confidently through the sand and removed the ball with it.

# Faults and fixes

## FAULT

### • Leaving the ball in the bunker

Many women golfers struggle with their bunker play because they are too delicate in their approach to the shot. It is not uncommon to see amateurs trying to remove their ball from the sand using nothing more than a waist-high backswing, in the mistaken belief that a bunker shot is similar to a chip shot. Not surprisingly, the ball rarely comes flying out positively and, more often than not, it remains in the bunker.

## FIX

### • Commit to a full backswing

When hitting bunker shots you must remember that there is a lot of loft on the face of your sand wedge, your stance is open (aiming left of the target) and that the sand is heavy. These factors combined make it very difficult to hit the ball a long way. With that in mind, it is vital that you take almost a full backswing, even from fairly short range. It is also worth remembering that the splash shot should be played with some aggression too. You need to accelerate the clubhead purposefully through the sand if you want to generate forward momentum on the ball.

## FAULT

### • Inconsistent strikes

Bunker play is one of the few areas of the game where you do not have to be too precise with your strike. You can hit 2.5–7cm (1–3in) behind the ball and still achieve roughly the same result. A shot where you take just an inch of sand will fly further but stop quicker once it lands on the green, while the shot where you take more sand will not travel as far, but will roll further on landing due to the lack of backspin. The reason why most golfers struggle with their bunker play is that they address the ball incorrectly and aim too squarely to the target.

## FIX

### • Draw a 'V' shape in the sand

To remind yourself of the correct swing path, draw two lines in the sand the next time you practice. Draw one line from the ball towards the target and the other aiming about 20 degrees to the left so that the two together form a 'V' shape. Aim the clubface along the right hand line and set your feet on the left hand line. Now swing up and down along the line of your feet as though you are going to hit the ball well left of the target. You will soon realize that you can swing to the left and the ball will still travel straight and true.

# *Putting*

**Y**ou may never be able to strike the ball as far as the likes of Karrie Webb or Laura Davies, but there is no reason why you cannot match them stroke for stroke on the green. Putting does not require any great athleticism, hand-eye coordination or strength; all that is needed is a good understanding of the technique and a feel for distance.

The average high handicapper takes at least 40 putts per round, while even the low handicap amateur will probably take 32 or 33. Compare those figures with the statistics of a top professional who will average somewhere in the region of 27 or 28 putts per round. Even taking into account the fact that the pros often hit putts from much closer range, it is a huge difference in the total for what basically involves hitting the ball along the ground over a fairly short distance.

In this chapter we will look at everything you need to become a good putter, from forming your grip to reading greens. If you can devote the same amount of time to working on your putting as you do to your long game, you will notice a satisfying improvement in your handicap.

# The putting set-up

It is often said that there is more room for individuality in putting than any other area of the game. However, although you see a variety of weird and wonderful putting styles demonstrated successfully on Tour, you must remember that the top players have developed an enhanced sense of touch through experience and regular practice. If your quirky stroke with all its glorious idiosyncrasies serves you well, fine, do not change a thing, but if you are prone to bouts of inconsistency

then it is probably time to give your putting stroke an overhaul, starting with a review of the basics.

Putting is not rocket science. It involves hitting the ball along the ground using a fairly short stroke; back and through. As with the full swing, your putting routine starts by aiming the club carefully at your intended line. Once you have done that correctly, you can then build the rest of your stance around the alignment of the putter face.

**1** Posture is as important in putting as it is in the long game. Stand relatively tall and create sharp angles with your spine and legs so that your arms can hang freely from your shoulders. For maximum consistency, your forearms and the putter should form a straight line.

**2** To give yourself the best possible view of the line of the putt, your eyes need to be directly over the ball. You can check this by dropping another ball from the top of your nose or by hanging your putter vertically from your eyes to see if it covers the ball. Forearms and putter should form a straight line.

## Putting Set-up Pointers

- Keep your eyes directly over the ball for the best view of the line of the putt
- Play the ball just forward of centre in your stance
- Create athletic angles with your posture so that you have a solid base to your stroke
- Forearms and shaft of putter form a straight line

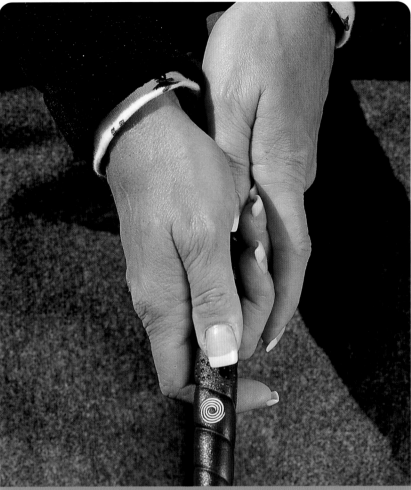

## THE REVERSE OVERLAP GRIP

**3** The putter face should stay low to the ground during the stroke. To avoid hitting down too steeply through impact, play the ball just forward of your sternum (chest bone), as this is just beyond the base point of the stroke and will, therefore, enable you to make contact with the ball slightly on the upswing, which is essential for imparting top spin.

Most golfers, amateur and professional, use a slightly different grip for putting than for hitting full shots. This is because the role of the hands in putting is significantly different than for the golf swing. When you hit a full shot, a certain amount of wrist action is required to create power and to get the ball in the air, but in putting very little power is needed. The ball remains on the ground and the wrists are virtually redundant.

The reverse overlap, which most professionals use when putting, is very similar to the regular overlapping grip shown earlier in the book, with the one exception that the left index finger extends down the shaft and rests on top of the last three fingers of the right hand. The purpose of this slight amendment is to allow the hands to work more as a unit on the grip, thereby reducing the tendency for the wrists to break during the stroke.

# *The putting stroke*

The putting stroke is a simple action as long as you adhere to a few ground rules. Firstly, keep your wrists out of the stroke at all costs. Flicking at the ball with the wrists to get it moving is a common fault, but it makes it difficult to control the pace and direction of the putt. Secondly, do not pick the putter up steeply in the backswing, as this will make you hit down through impact, causing the ball to skid along the grass.

Most top golfers control their putting stroke with either arms or shoulders. I recommend you use both. The shoulders control the stroke, while the arms add feel to help you judge distance on long putts. Swing the putter away, keeping the clubhead low to the ground, and maintain the 'Y' shape formed by the forearms and shaft. The lower body must remain as still as possible to maximize your chances of a solid strike.

## *Match the length of the stroke to the length of the putt*

Once you feel comfortable with the basic putting stroke motion, you can start working on the pace and length of the stroke. As a rule, the putter will swing straight back and through on fairly short putts, but move slightly inside the line as the length of putt increases.

Always keep in mind that it is the length of the stroke that determines how far you hit the ball. Many golfers make the mistake of trying to speed up their stroke when faced with a long-range putt, but by speeding up, their timing and ball striking goes awry. The secret is to keep an even-paced tempo to your stroke and simply increase or decrease the length of your stroke to hit the ball different distances.

**1** Keep your lower body and your head perfectly still and glide the putter away from the ball low to the ground, with your arms and shoulders working together as a unit.

**2** Maintain the 'Y' shape formed between your arms and the shaft of the putter at address all the way through the hitting area and into your follow-through. Your head should remain steady throughout.

## Putting Pointers

- Keep the putter's face low to the ground during the stroke
- Swing the putter with your arms and shoulders
- Keep your hands and wrists out of the shot – do not flick at the ball
- Increase the length of the stroke to hit the ball further

## KEEP THE PUTTER FACE BELOW THE BALL

Many putting problems are caused by hitting down too steeply on the ball as a result of playing it too far back in the stance. Picking the putter up in the air on the backswing can also lead to this fault. By hitting down, the player reduces the loft on the putter and drives the ball into the ground. The inevitable result is that the ball then pops up into the air and diverts from its intended line. To produce a smooth roll with plenty of top spin, the putter should approach the ball at a shallow angle. A good way to ensure such an approach, is to keep the putter face below the top of the ball throughout the stroke; this will keep your putter hugging the ground as it approaches the ball at the correct angle.

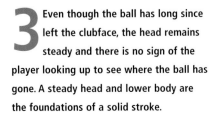

**3** Even though the ball has long since left the clubface, the head remains steady and there is no sign of the player looking up to see where the ball has gone. A steady head and lower body are the foundations of a solid stroke.

# Faults and fixes

## FAULT

## FIX

### • Missing short putts

There is nothing more frustrating than missing a short putt. There are three main causes of this problem: careless alignment; a hesitant stroke; and excessive head movement.

To stand over a short putt with confidence you need to know that you are aiming the putter face on the correct line. An uncertain alignment will be reflected in a nervous and tentative stroke. Another killer fault is looking up too early to see whether you have holed the putt. This may sound like an innocuous habit, but its effects are significant. Looking up after you have struck the ball is fine, but, if you begin the process of looking towards the hole in your downswing, your whole upper body will move out of line, causing you to drag the ball left.

### • Aim dead centre and keep your head steady

On short-range putts, a good strategy is to aim at the centre of the hole and stroke the putt firmly to reduce the break. By doing this, you give yourself a couple of inches margin for error either side of the target, and this will help compensate for any slight error with the putter face alignment or a little extra break.

There are two main ways you can prevent yourself from looking up too early. The first is to focus on a point behind the ball at address and continue to stare at it until the putter has struck the ball. You will often see professionals look down at the ball until it has travelled several feet. Alternatively, ask a friend to hold your head steady as you hit some putts.

| FAULT | FIX |
|---|---|

### • Too much wrist action leads to poor distance control

Many frustrating three-putts are caused by poor distance control on the first long-range attempt. One of the main reasons behind this lack of control on the greens is a simple lack of play. The other – and far more damaging – contributing factor is that many golfers feel that they need to flick at the ball with their wrists to get it moving towards the hole, rather than allowing the swinging motion of the putter to do the work.

If your timing is spot-on you can occasionally get away with unhinging your wrists through impact, but more often than not, the uncontrolled release of the wrists plays havoc with your accuracy and tempo.

### • Keep your right wrist firm to avoid the flick

A good practice exercise to help you avoid a breakdown of the wrists through impact, is to focus on holding the angle formed at the back of your right wrist all the way through the stroke from start to finish.

Holding the putter with just your right hand, focus on the angle at the back of your right wrist and then hit some practice putts, concentrating purely on maintaining that angle all the way through the stroke. Once you have successfully completed the practice stroke several times, recreate the same feelings in your stroke for real.

# *Reading greens*

Although a fluent putting stroke is an enviable attribute, even more important is the ability to read greens. It is very rare to find a totally flat lie on any putting surface, so you will invariably need to aim either to the left or right of the hole to allow for the contours. The amount that the ball curves on the slope is known as the 'break' or 'borrow'. Accurately judging the speed of putts and to what extent the ball will break is a talent that separates the truly great putters from the merely average player.

Reading greens is a skill that you acquire through playing at a variety of different courses, on different types of grasses and in different climates. However, there are a few basic practices that will set you on the right road. Firstly, the harder you hit a putt the less it will break. That is why uphill putts break less than downhill ones. At the same time, most putts break more as they slow down toward the hole. A ball will also break more on a dry green, where there is less resistance than on a wet green where the water slows the ball down.

**1** Take your first look at the putt from behind the ball to get your initial impression of the way the ball will break. If necessary, crouch down low for a better view.

**2** Walk to a point midway between the ball and the hole on the low side to get a more accurate idea of the distance. If you only look at the putt from behind you often get a foreshortened view and underestimate the length.

**3** Although you get a better view of the putt from the low side as the ball will break towards you, it is still worth taking a look at the putt from the other side as you walk back to your ball.

### Green-reading Pointers

- Start to read a green as you approach it from the fairway
- Uphill putts break less than downhill putts
- Always view a long putt from the side to get an accurate perspective of the distance involved
- View putts from several angles for best results

**4** Many top golfers, and particularly Americans, plum-bob to read greens. This involves hanging the putter vertically in line with the centre of the hole to see which side is higher and, therefore, how the ball will break.

## QUICK TIP

### Make your practice putts parallel to your intended line

Once you have decided on the line of a putt, committing yourself to that line is absolutely crucial. Get into the habit of making your practice putts parallel to your intended line rather than at the hole itself. That way, it will not feel so strange when you stand over the ball and swing away from the hole.

# Course Management

**T**he ability to think your way around the golf course in a sensible manner is vital to good scoring. However, 'course management,' to use the technical term, is often underestimated. The world's top players seldom waste shots. They are master tacticians and experts at squeezing every last drop of potential out of their round. Make it your goal to be as prudent. Thinking smart means planning ahead, analyzing the best way to negotiate a hole while playing to your strengths and minimizing risks.

Course management is also about knowing your limitations, keeping a check on your ego and being able to decide when to take on the risky recovery and when to opt for the safe percentage shot. For many women, good course management and strategy can often help compensate for a lack of power off the tee and from the fairway. If you can keep the ball out of trouble and play to your strengths, you will eliminate the disaster scores from your card and keep your round ticking over.

# Pre-round preparation

At a basic level, good course management can be as simple as knowing how far you hit each club, or using your favourite iron off the tee when you are feeling nervous. At the other end of the scale, low handicappers and professionals will often shape their shots in a specific way off the tee to set up easier approach shots into the green.

However, nothing is guaranteed to ruin a score faster than arriving at the golf course with just a few minutes to spare before your tee-off time. Take a leaf out of the professionals' book and, where possible, always try to arrive 45 minutes before you are due to begin your round.

## Allow plenty of time to reach the golf course

Think of your pre-match or competition routine as starting the moment you wake up in the morning. Make sure that you remain calm throughout the day and leave your house in plenty of time to take a slow drive to the golf course. The last thing you need is the stress of getting caught in traffic and wondering whether or not you will arrive in time to play. Once you get to the club, check-in, get changed and make sure that you have everything that you will need on the first tee before you go out to the course to warm up.

It is a good idea to spend at least 15 minutes on the practice range to loosen your muscles and get a feel for your swing. This is not the time to make big changes to your swing. Accept that the shots you are hitting will remain with you for the day. Start with your wedges, work your way up through the bag until you are warmed up and ready to hit a few fairway woods and drives. Finish your warm-up session with a few wedge shots again to restore your rhythm.

You should also hit a few long-range putts to test the pace of the greens and hole a few really short putts to boost your confidence before you head to the first tee.

*Above left:* **Make time to hit a few long-range putts on the practice green before you play so that you can improve your touch and acclimatize to the pace of the greens.**

*Left:* **Always hole two or three short-range putts before you leave the practice putting green so that you feel confident as you head to the first tee.**

### *Preparation Pointers*
- Allow enough time for a relaxed drive to the course
- Spend at least 15 minutes warming up your swing
- Start and finish your warm-up by hitting some wedge shots
- Hit some long-range putts to test the pace of the greens
- Always hole a short putt

## *Your opening tee shot sets the tone for the day*

The first tee shot of the day is the most important of the round. Hit a fantastic shot straight down the middle and you feel that you can take on the world. Fluff the shot, however, and it is easy to get despondent, lose confidence and allow your game to go from bad to worse.

### Adhere to sensible first tee strategies

There are several ways to improve your chances of starting your round in a positive manner. First, make sure that you are ready before you head to the first tee. The opening tee shot of any round can be nerve-wracking enough without introducing unnecessary tension and anxiety by having to rummage around in your golf bag to find some tees or a ball. Without any distractions, you can devote all your concentration to striking the ball.

Secondly, there is no rule that says you have to hit a driver or 3-wood off the first tee. Ignore any peer pressure. If you are feeling nervous, select your favourite club for the opening shot; even if that means hitting a 7-iron. A well-struck mid-iron that travels 130yds straight down the centre of the fairway will do far more for your confidence than a pathetically struck shot into the trees with a driver.

Finally, another good ploy that the top players will use when they are feeling the pressure standing on the tee is to slow down the pre-shot routine. When you are nervous, your body's natural instinct is to speed up to get the situation over and done with as soon as possible. However, rushing is a recipe for disaster in golf, so make a conscious effort to take your time over the preparation of the shot.

## *QUICK TIP*

### *Make full use of the teeing area*

The rules of golf allow you to tee the ball anywhere within the rectangle that stretches back two club lengths between the tee box markers. Many golfers walk straight out onto the middle of the teeing area to hit their tee shot without a second's thought. However, you should consider the shot you want to hit, look for the hazards on the hole and then choose the most appropriate position from which to hit your tee shot. Choosing to hit the ball from either the left or right side of the tee markers will often increase your landing area in the fairway and, therefore, give you more confidence.

# Tee shot strategies

## Par-3: Aim for the back of the green or the widest landing area

The greens on par-3 holes tend to be well guarded, thereby placing a premium on the accuracy of your tee shot. However, if you look closely, in most cases, virtually all of the trouble on short holes is at the front of the green. It is rare to find bunkers and water hazards behind the putting surface, so select a club that enables you to reach the back of the green. Even if you mishit the shot slightly, you still have a chance of ending up pin-high or on the front portion of the green, not in the sand or a lake.

Another point worth noting is that on very short holes, the green-keeper will often cut the hole in a tricky position; just behind a bunker or on the narrowest part of the green. These are known as 'sucker pins', as only suckers aim at them. In such a situation, it is a good idea to aim for the widest and deepest portion of the green and look to make a safe par.

## Par-4: Look for the trouble off the tee

Have you ever noticed how a tee shot that is heading for a fairway bunker always has just enough strength to trickle into the sand? You may think you are just plain unlucky, but there is more to it than simple misfortune. The course designers have done plenty of research and know your game just as well as you do, which is why they will always place at least one hazard on the hole in the most common landing area to catch errant tee shots. Normally, these take the form of fairway bunkers, water or trees, although mounding and rough are also commonly used to make life difficult for you.

The key to good scoring on a par-4, regardless of its length, is to avoid the trouble that lurks around the landing area of your drives. Before you tee the ball up, take a look at the layout of the hole and note the position of the hazards. If they are in range, then either select a club that will leave your ball comfortably short of the danger, or alternatively aim well away from the hazards.

## Par-5: Analyse the hole before reaching for your driver

Many golfers think that a par-5 is a license to reach straight for the driver off the tee. However, that is not always a smart decision. Your first thought should be to determine whether or not the hole is reachable in two shots. If so, hitting the driver may well be a calculated risk worth taking. If, however, the hole plays as a genuine three-shotter, as par-5s usually do for most women, then you have to think carefully about what you will actually gain from using the longest and least-forgiving club in your bag. Why risk hitting the driver followed by a fairway wood and a pitching wedge when three 5-irons will get you to the green more comfortably?

One particular strategy that top professionals use on long par-5s is the lay-up. If they cannot reach the green with their second shot, instead of trying to get the ball as close as possible to the hole, and leaving themselves an awkward length pitch shot, they purposely leave themselves a full shot into the green with their favourite club, which is normally a pitching wedge or a 9-iron. Laying up is not a negative tactic if it allows you stand over the ball feeling positive about your approach shot.

### Tee shot strategies

- Take full advantage of the teeing ground and think carefully about where you should tee the ball to give you the best line on the hole.
- Determine the position of hazards on the hole around the landing area and adjust your club selection and aim accordingly.
- Have a game plan for every hole. Work backwards from the green to the tee in order to work out how you should hit your tee shot.
- Play to your strengths. If you are a long-hitter, you may benefit from trying to reach the green on a very short par-4. On the other hand, if you are a good wedge player you will probably benefit more by playing an iron or fairway wood from the tee so that you leave yourself your favourite distance from the pin.
- Take the wind direction into account when planning your tee shots. In warm weather your ball will fly further than in cold temperatures.
- Only use your driver if you know that the benefits outweigh the risks. More often than not a 3-wood or a 5-wood off the tee will hit the ball just as far and much straighter.
- If you are a higher handicapper or beginner, allow for mishits off the tee by taking at least one extra club on par-3s. This strategy will also help you avoid hazards placed in front of the green.
- Play your own game. Never try to out-drive an opponent or fellow competitor.

# Playing the percentages

## Make a bogey your worst score

One of golf's golden rules is that if you are not confident about your ability to play a particular shot, do not play it. Nowhere is this advice more relevant than when you have missed the fairway and are amongst the trees. For whatever reason, golfers seem to lose their ability to think rationally in these situations. Instead of accepting that the most sensible course of action is to get the ball safely back in play on the fairway, where you will have a clear route to the green, most amateurs still attempt to play the miracle recovery shot. On

most occasions, the player is left in even deeper trouble after their failed attempt at glory.

When temptation is getting the better of you, give yourself an ego-check. The top players know that the fastest way to run up a big score on any hole is to compound an error with several more. Pars and bogeys add up slowly on the scorecard, but double and triple bogeys can very quickly ruin a round. Although it may feel boring to chip sideways onto the fairway, it is better to drop just one shot than to run the risk of wasting several more.

**1** When assessing a shot out of the rough or the trees, by all means consider the adventurous recovery shot, but be realistic about your chances of playing the shot successfully. In most instances, the risks will inevitably outweigh the rewards.

**2** If you decide that the best course of action is to chip out sideways or punch your ball forwards, make sure that you get the ball out and well clear of the trouble. Commit fully to the shot so that you can definitely play your next approach from the fairway.

## *On course strategies*

- Only attempt an adventurous recovery shot if you know that you have a better than 50 per cent chance of playing it successfully.
- Do not take risks when laying up short of hazards. Always select a club that will leave your ball comfortably short, even if you strike it perfectly.
- From poor lies in bunkers and the rough, be satisfied with getting the ball safely on the green or back on the fairway.
- Learn from watching your playing partner's shots.
- Be observant at all times. Check for hazards off the tee and look for the trouble around the green.
- Never attempt to play a complicated shot when a simple one will do the job just as well – if not even better.
- Focus on the shot you want to play, not the swing you want to make. Always visualize a shot in your mind before playing it.

*Below:* If your playing partner's ball lies on a similar line, you can learn a lot by watching how their putt breaks as it runs out of pace around the hole.

## *Watch playing partners putt*

Amateur golfers are notorious for wasting shots on the greens. One reason for this is that they are generally unobservant and fail to fully utilize the resources that are available to them. We have looked at the intricacies of reading greens earlier in the book, but if after viewing the putt from a couple of angles you are still unsure about how it will break then take the time to observe your playing partner's putts.

Although this is obviously of greater benefit to you if your partner's ball is on a similar line, you can still learn a lot from putts that approach the hole from the opposite side. It is particularly useful to note how the ball moves during the last couple of feet as it slows down, as this will give you an idea of how your own putt will break around the hole.

# Distance judgement

## Playing in the wind

Windy conditions intimidate many women golfers because they feel that they do not have the power to combat the elements, particularly when playing into a strong headwind. In this testing situation, it is very easy to fall into the trap of swinging harder and faster. However, when you do this you impart more backspin on the ball, it flies higher than normal and is likely to meet greater resistance from the wind.

The good news is that you do not have to increase your swing speed, power or technique to overcome the wind. On full shots, all you need to do is take an extra club and swing more rhythmically than usual. When judging how the strength of the wind will affect the flight of the ball, most top golfers talk in 'clubs'. A 'two-club' wind is one that will require the player to hit a 5-iron to carry the ball the same distance as their 7-iron would in still conditions. Judging the wind is obviously a skill that comes with experience, but the concept of hitting at least one extra club rather than simply swinging faster will undoubtedly help your game.

Finally, remember to always swing more rhythmically than normal when playing into the wind. While swinging faster increases the amount of backspin you impart on the ball and in turn the height of the shot, swinging more gently reduces the amount of backspin generated, leading to a lower, more penetrating ball flight that is less susceptible to the effects of the wind.

**1** To hit a lower shot into the wind, play the ball just back of centre in your stance, and set up with your weight slightly favouring your front foot. This will 'de-loft' the clubface at address and help you keep the ball low.

**2** Stay centred over the ball as you make a three-quarter length backswing. Keep your tempo smooth and controlled. You may want to choke down on the grip a few inches for extra control over the shot and to reduce loft.

**3** Make sure that your hands lead the clubface and remain ahead of the ball through impact. If the clubhead overtakes your hands through the hitting area, you will add loft to the clubface and the ball will fly higher.

## Distance Pointers

- Slow your swing down when playing into the wind since swinging faster will produce a higher shot
- Regularly assess your yardages so that you know how far you hit the ball with any given club
- Just because you once carried the ball 160yds with a 5-iron does not make it your normal yardage with that club

## KNOW YOUR YARDAGES

In addition to the 100yd, 150yd and 200yd marker posts found on the fairways, many golf courses supply stroke saver guides and display exact yardages to the green on the sprinkler heads dotted around the fairways. With so much information at your disposal, there is no excuse for not knowing how far it is to the hole from virtually any position. However, the knowledge that you have, for example, 153yds to the centre of the green is useless if you do not know how far you hit the ball with each club in your bag. For a sport that places such a premium on distance control, it is amazing how many golfers have absolutely no idea how far they hit the ball with any given club.

All it takes is half an hour or so of practice time to work out your average yardage with each club. The key is to remember that you are looking for your average yardage, not your best shot. To work out your yardages, hit ten balls with each club. Ignore your two best shots and your two worst, then take an average of the remaining six balls. Like it or not, that is your yardage. Keep a written note of the results for reference and, if possible, frequently update them, particularly if you are having regular lessons.

On the course, use your personal yardages as the starting point for your club selection. However, factors such as sloping lies and wind may require you to revise your club selection. Playing downhill, for example, means that the ball will stay in the air longer, so you will usually need to take a more lofted club. For an uphill shot, the elevated green means that the ball will not complete its normal full flight and will land earlier, so you will need to take at least one club more.

**4** Because your hands have been kept well ahead of the ball through impact, your follow-through will automatically be abbreviated when playing a punch shot into the wind. Avoid hinging your wrists in the follow-through.

# Effective Practice

**M**ore inquisitive readers may wonder why this chapter is called 'effective practice' rather than just 'practice'. The reason is simple, because practice is actually anything but effective for most amateur golfers. If your idea of a productive practice session is to head down to your local driving range and aimlessly hit 100 balls with a driver as quickly as possible, sadly I must inform you that you are exercising, not practising.

Regular practice will play an essential role in your progress as a golfer, and it is very important that you set time aside on a regular basis to develop your game. However, most amateurs have neither the time nor the inclination to devote countless hours of their spare time to practice, so the emphasis should always be on quality rather than quantity. Half an hour of concentrated and focused work is far more beneficial than several hours spent bashing drivers into the distance.

In this chapter you will learn how to structure your practice sessions and work on all areas of your game more efficiently so that you can make maximum progress in the shortest amount of time.

*Left:* When working on your long game, always build a practice station so that you can hit every shot from the correct address position. This will give you accurate feedback on shots.

*Below:* While introducing a major change into your swing, it is a good idea to make plenty of practice swings without a ball so that you get used to the new feelings and positions.

## Groove your address position

The first step when working on your swing or long game should be to build a practice station. One of the bases of a good practice session is hitting every shot from a consistent address position. If you are working on your swing, for example, and never stand to the ball in the same way twice, you will struggle to get good feedback on your improvement.

Pick out a target to aim at and then lay a club on the ground parallel to your target line between the ball and your feet. Now place another club between your feet at right angles to the shaft on the ground to monitor the ball position. The two clubs should create a 'T' shape, which can be used as an alignment guide to ensure that you aim your body and the clubface correctly, while retaining a consistent ball position.

Another benefit of using a practice station is that it forces you to focus on a target. Many amateurs fall into the trap of standing on the practice range hitting balls aimlessly out onto the grass, but this is a very bad habit to acquire. If you do not aim at a target, you will not get any true feedback on how accurate your shots are, and you can kid yourself into thinking that you are hitting good shots when in fact they are well off

line. You will invariably transfer the same, sloppy attitude from the driving range onto the golf course, where errant shots will land in trees, bunkers and rough.

Practice sessions should replicate the situations you find yourself in on a golf course. You aim for a flag on the green when playing for real, so get into the habit of doing the same thing at the driving range.

## Develop technique and routine

Practice sessions have two main purposes: to improve and refine your techniques, and to develop and groove a consistent pre-shot routine. Ideally, you should go through your whole routine with every practice shot, but if you do not have time for that, make sure that you focus on your routine on at least two out of ten practice balls you hit.

While working on your swing technique, make plenty of practice swings away from the ball and hit fewer shots. The reason for this is that you can quickly become disheartened if you do not see good results instantly, and there will be a temptation to revert back to your old tried and trusted swing simply to see the ball fly somewhere toward the target.

## *Practice Pointers*

- **Build a practice station to groove a good address position**
- **Always aim at a target to improve your focus**
- **Hit less balls, make more practice swings**
- **Set aside time to develop a pre-shot routine**
- **Practise your weaknesses as well as your strengths**
- **Devise a practice schedule and plan**

When you introduce a change to your swing, it is likely that the quality of your shots will suffer to some degree in the short term as your body and timing adjust to the new positions and feelings. The key, though, is to feel the movements you want to achieve in your swing. Make several rehearsals of the motion away from the ball and then hit a practice shot focusing on the same feelings.

# *Target your weaknesses*

It is human nature to practise things we are already good at, but unfortunately, your handicap will never improve if you constantly neglect the less accomplished parts of your game. If you are a strong wedge player, for example, it is tempting to spend most of your practice time working on these shots because it makes you feel good and gives your confidence a boost. In reality, though, your time would be better spent working on, say, your long irons or fairway woods.

When you go to the driving range, you should apply yourself to the job in hand. You can even consider leaving your favourite clubs at home to avoid temptation and force yourself to work on the weaknesses in your game.

An effective plan is to devote a certain amount of time per week to all areas of your game, and then make extra time available for your weaknesses. Rather than ranking your wedge play at nine out of ten and your fairway woods at only two out of ten, for example, aim to score at least seven out of ten for both.

## *QUICK TIP*

### *Check set-up in front of a mirror*

One of the best ways to work on your swing basics – and many areas of the full swing itself – is to rehearse your posture and general set-up in front of a large mirror. You can either do this at home or at the driving range, where many of the bays are fitted with full-length mirrors to help you monitor your swing.

A mirror gives you immediate feedback on the quality of your address position. The downside is that there is nowhere to hide and it can be a harsh taskmaster. Do not be surprised to discover that what you thought was the ideal posture is rather less impressive in the flesh. However, you will quickly be able to make dramatic improvements to your set-up using the mirror to help monitor your positions.

# Putting practice

Putting is one area of the game where a little practice can make an enormous difference to your scores and your handicap. There are three key areas you need to focus on when working on putting: reading the greens; your technique; and your distance control.

## Reading greens

Reading greens is an invaluable skill, yet hardly any golfers – even low handicappers – bother to practice it. To test your proficiency in this part of the game, find a medium- to long-range putt with a fair amount of break. Now go through your green reading routine (see p104) and, once you have finished analyzing the putt, place a tee peg in the green at the point you believe the ball will begin to curve back to the hole. Hit a few practice putts aiming at the tee and check to see if you have judged the borrow correctly. It is my guess that for the first few attempts you will underestimate the amount of break. Repeat the exercise until your judgement becomes more accurate. For best results, vary the length of each putt and practise as many left-to-right putts as right-to-lefters.

## QUICK TIP

### Practice putts with different breaks to hone your skills

When practising reading greens, spend time working on different kinds of putts. Many golfers will favour one type of breaking putt over another. However, make sure that you devote as much time to practising the putts that you don't like so that you are confident of dealing with any kind of breaking putt on the course.

*Above right and right:* Check your green-reading skills by placing a tee peg in the ground at the point you believe the ball will begin to curve back toward the hole. Aim at the tee and check to see if you have read the green correctly.

*Right:* Groove your technique from short range by ensuring that your stroke stays within the two clubs laid either side of the hole.

*Below:* Learning to strike the ball firmly enough to finish past the hole is the first step to learning distance control from long range.

## Technique

Most women's putting practice is limited to hitting just a few short putts before a round to build confidence and a couple of long-range attempts to improve their sense of touch and feel. The problem with that routine is that it ignores the medium-range putts of 10–20ft, and these are the putts that highlight the flaws in your stroke.

A good way to work on your stroke is to find a flat part of the practice green and then, starting from about 2ft from the hole, hit three putts. Once you hole all three in succession, move a few feet further away and attempt to hole all three putts until you reach 15ft away. The beauty of the exercise is that it immediately highlights your problem distances and the faults in your stroke. Do not be surprised if this is sooner rather than later. While you may be able to hole the two- and three-footers comfortably, the flaws in your stroke will start to show from around five feet out. If you hole out regularly from 5ft to 10ft you will notice a big difference in your scores.

## Distance control

Even the world's best golfers do not expect to hole many 30–40ft putts. What they do expect, though, is to lag the ball right up to the holeside for a safe tap-in. Controlling the distance on your approach putts is the key to success on the greens. Most of your soul-destroying three-putts will originate from leaving the first putt several feet short of the hole. Eliminate those tentative strokes and you will save at least three or four shots per round.

A good way to become more authoritative with your putting is to create a box behind a hole with three clubs and then, from 30–40ft, attempt to roll every putt into that box. What this does is take your attention away from the hole and instead allow your mind to focus purely on the distance. If you can roll the ball into this zone every time, you will never leave yourself more than a couple of feet away from the hole. You can even take that image onto the golf course with you and use it when you face a long-range putt.

# *Chipping practice*

Your short game will need regular fine-tuning to keep it at a consistently high standard. There are an infinite number of different situations you can find yourself in around the greens, so much of your practice time must be spent on developing touch, feel and imagination as well as a consistent technique.

## *Hole out after every chip shot*

One of the most common mistakes made by amateurs when working on their short game is to hit lots of chip shots onto the practice green, but never complete the job by holing the putt. Practice should recreate on-course situations as closely as possible. The danger with hitting one shot after another, even though you may be concentrating fully on what you are

doing, is that complacency inevitably creeps in at some stage. If one of your practice chip shots rolls 6ft past the hole, instead of being disappointed as you would be on the golf course, you think nothing of it and immediately get the next practice ball and have another go. Unfortunately, you do not have that luxury on the golf course.

If you never finish the job by holing your putts, you will never find out how good you really are at chipping. Getting up and down in two when it counts is often just as much about your mental resilience as it is your touch and technique. If you have played every chip shot for real in practice, you stand much more chance of hitting the ball close when you find yourself facing a similar shot in a competition.

**1** Although it is tempting to stand on the edge of the green and hit chip shot after chip shot onto the putting surface to develop your touch, you should restrict yourself to hitting six practice shots before walking onto the green and holing each one out.

**2** In an ideal world, every chip shot would finish right next to the hole, but more often than not, you will leave yourself a putt of 2–6ft in length. The ability to hole out from this distance is almost as important as the chip shot itself.

## Learn how to land the ball first bounce on the green every time

The secret to good chipping is selecting a club that will land the ball first bounce on the green and run the rest of the way to the hole. A good exercise to help you judge your chip shots more accurately is to lay two clubs on the green about 3ft apart, placing either a small coin or a credit card in the middle as your target to land the ball on.

With the target in place, you can hit practice chip shots with a variety of different clubs, attempting each time to land the ball within the guideline of the clubs each time. You will soon begin to notice that if you hit your sand wedge to land the ball on the coin or card, the ball will not roll as far as when you use one of your straighter-faced clubs, such as a 5-iron or a 6-iron. This will not only teach you the lengths of swings needed to get the ball onto the green, but also the different performance characteristics of each club. By the end of the session you will be able to make a better decision on club selection when faced with a chip shot on the golf course.

### PRACTISE WITH A FRIEND

Solitary practice can get rather monotonous after a while, at which point aimlessly hitting balls will probably do your game more harm than good. To maintain your concentration and add a bit of spark to your practice sessions, challenge a like-minded friend to a small competition. Nothing heightens your awareness and improves your concentration more than a little light-hearted one-on-one. You will be amazed at how quickly you react to the challenge and find yourself focusing intently on every shot.

*Above left and left:* By aiming to land the ball on a target positioned a few feet onto the green, you will learn the length of swing needed to clear the fringe grass and the performance characteristics of each club in your bag for chipping.

# *Bunker play practice*

Together with pitching, bunker play is probably the least practised part of the game, so it is hardly surprising that most players never improve their technique and remain intimidated by the sand. Unfortunately, unless you are a member of a private golf club, good short game facilities are few and far between and you may have to rely on just a few minutes' time in the practice bunker at the golf course before you tee off. It is not ideal preparation, but a little practice is better than none whatsoever. Here are a few quick-fire practice exercises that you can use to fine-tune your bunker play.

## *Draw a 'V' shape to groove your swing path*

The key to solid bunker play is to understand that, in most cases, you never swing the club along the target line. Instead, your swing line should be several degrees left of the flag. This compensates for the fact that when you open the clubface to maximize the bounce angle on the sole, the club aims slightly to the right and also improves the performance of the sand wedge itself through impact.

No matter how adept you are from the sand, it is always worthwhile drawing a few lines in the practice bunker to remind you of the required swing path and clubface alignment. Find a nice flat lie and then draw a 'V' shape in the sand, with the top of each side of the letter aiming just to the left and the right of the hole respectively. The left line represents your body alignment, stance and swing path, while the right line represents where your clubface should be aiming. Remember, if you aim your body to the left, and the clubface slightly to the right, the ball will fly straight.

## *Learn to judge your point of entry into the sand*

A common cause of poor bunker play is taking too much sand before the ball. When you do this, two things can occur. Firstly, you may hit the ball too heavily and struggle to create enough swing speed to get it out of the bunker altogether. Alternatively, the clubface enters and exits the sand before it reaches the ball, leading either to an excessively heavy shot or causing the leading edge of your sand wedge to catch the ball in the middle and send it racing across the green at 100mph.

If you adhere to the bunker play checklist outlined on page 93, you will not have to worry about how much sand to take, since shuffling your feet into the bunker will lower the base point of your swing and enable you to slide the clubface under the ball. However, another way to improve the quality of your strike is to simply draw a straight line in the sand a couple of inches behind the ball and then make some practice swings, focusing on splashing the clubhead down into the sand directly on top of that line. You will probably be way out on your first few attempts, which may give you a clue as to why your bunker play is not quite as good as it should be. However, once you can strike the line consistently, you can place a ball about an inch or so ahead of the line and repeat the same exercise. You should see a remarkable improvement.

## Practise the difficult shots, too

Hitting a succession of practice shots from flat well-manicured sand in the bunker may help to develop your technique, touch and confidence, but it is unrealistic to expect to find such a perfect lie every time on the golf course. Bunkers can be busy places, and every so often you will find your ball lying in a foot print, or on scruffy unraked sand or tucked right against the front or back lip or even plugged completely.

Prepare yourself for worst case scenarios by attempting some of the more awkward shots in practice. At least that will give you a chance of extricating your ball from the back lip, or give you some idea of how to deal with a shot when you have to address the ball with your feet positioned outside the bunker, as often happens.

Once you have finished working on your standard bunker play technique, take a few minutes at the end of the session to try a few of the more awkward shots. Standing with your back to the bunker, take a dozen or so balls and throw them back over your head into the sand. Then go and play each one as it lies. Although you may struggle with a few, it is certainly a fun way to end your workout.

*Above left:* **Get into the habit of making at least a three-quarter length swing when playing a basic bunker shot.**

*Left:* **Commitment through the ball is one of the fundamentals of consistent and successful bunker play. Always accelerate the clubhead through the sand.**

*Right:* **Finish your short game and bunker play sessions by throwing a few balls over your head and then play each one as it lies.**

# *index*

# *acknowledgements*

The author and publishers would like to thank **East Sussex National Golf Club** and **Woburn Golf Club** for their friendliness, patience and superb facilities. We would also like to thank the models for giving their time and expertise amid difficult conditions.

Models: Alison Duff, Sarah MacLennan, Beverly Huke, Alison Brunsden and Claire Waite.
Swing sequence on pages 48–51: Carin Koch

**Executive Editor** Trevor Davies
**Editor** Sharon Ashman
**Senior Designer** Joanna Bennett
**Designer** Ginny Zeal
**Picture Research** Liz Fowler
**Production Controller** Viv Cracknell
**Special photography** Mark Newcombe

All the photographs in this book have been taken by Mark Newcombe for the Octopus Publishing Group Ltd, except for the following:
**Action Images**/John Sibley 85 right
**Allsport**/David Cannon 25 /Scott Halleran 24 /Craig Jones 13 Bottom /Andrew Redington 10–11, 23
**Golf Picture Bank**/Nick Walker 7, 99 right
**Phil Sheldon** 22
**Visions in Golf**/Mark Newcombe front cover bottom left, 48 top left, 48 top right, 48 bottom right, 48 bottom left, 49 bottom right, 49 right, 49 top left, 49 bottom left, 50 top left, 50 top right, 50 bottom right, 50 bottom left, 51 top left, 51 top right, 51 bottom right, 51 bottom left